Beginning the Journey

Entering the Kingdom of God

RALPH W. NEIGHBOUR, JR.
AND JIM EGLI

TOUCH PUBLICATIONS
Houston, Texas, U.S.A.

Beginning the Journey

Published by TOUCH Publications
P.O. Box 19888 • Houston, Texas, 77224-9888, U.S.A.
(281) 497-7901 • Fax (281) 497-0904

International Standard Book Number: 1-880828-29-4

TOUCH Publications is the book-publishing division of
TOUCH Outreach Ministries, a resource and consulting
ministry for churches with a vision for cell-based local
church structure.

Find us on the World Wide Web at
http://www.touchusa.org

TABLE OF CONTENTS

Note: A sheet of Scripture memory verses is bound in at the back of this booklet. Cut them apart and carry them with you, memorizing the six Scripture verses.

Unit 1, Day 1
Welcome To Your New Journey!

GETTING STARTED

Congratulations on your decision to follow Jesus Christ! As you begin the exciting journey of life with Him, this book will encourage and guide you. Think of this book as a trail guide that will lead you to explore your new path in Christ.

Over the next year, you'll take an equipping journey that will help you experience God's love and prepare you for a lifetime of ministry to others. Right now you are taking the first steps of your trip. After completing this part of the journey, you will take the next steps which will help you examine your values in life and walk in daily victory with Christ. Beyond that, other studies will teach you how to share Christ's love with others.

HOW TO USE THIS BOOK

This booklet is divided into five units. Each week as you complete a unit, you will meet with your mentor to go over what you have learned. Your mentor is someone from your cell group who is ahead of you on his or her journey. Your mentor will encourage you, pray for you, and help you to grow. A *Mentor's Guide,* located in the back of this book, will direct him or her in leading your times together. Often these times will be the high point of your week, giving you and your mentor an opportunity to encourage one another as you grow in Christ together.

Each unit in this booklet has daily growth guides. There are five in each week. You'll discover exciting truths about yourself and your relationship to Christ as you go through these daily guides. The guides use an interactive format with questions for you to answer or responses for you to check whenever you see this symbol:

 So keep a pen or pencil at hand. These questions will help you dig into the Scripture and apply it to your own life.

THE POWER OF SCRIPTURE MEMORY

As you grow in Christ, you'll discover that the Bible is a powerful resource for strengthening your life and giving you direction. Memorizing key Scriptures gives you ready access to the riches of God's Word. It equips you to repel the attacks and temptations of Satan. The evil one isn't happy about your decision to follow Christ and he will try to divert and hinder your growth. You may have noticed that he is already trying!

When he tries to pull you off course through temptation or deception, God's Word can keep you on track. Jesus' own example in Matthew 4 shows us the power of Scripture to conquer the evil one. When Satan tempted Jesus, our Lord repeatedly quoted God's Word to win a decisive victory.

It's easy to memorize Scriptures when you keep them handy and use any free moments to review them. When you commit God's Word to memory, you have ready access to it — even when you aren't near a Bible!

You can review the verses each day whenever you have extra moments — like when you are waiting in a line or stopped at a red light. In the next year, you will memorize many powerful verses. They will nourish you and help you as you share your faith in Christ with family and friends.

Your first memory verse is 1 John 5:11-12. It reads:

"And this is the testimony: God has given us eternal life, and this life is in his Son. He who has the Son has the life; he who does not have the Son of God does not have the life."

Your new journey is the journey of life. You don't have to wait until you get to heaven to enjoy the fruit of this life. God gave you life on the same day you gave your heart to Christ. From now on, you can experience this new life that is both joyful and exciting.

According to 1 John 5:11-12, what is the key to life?

_____

_____

Jesus is the Son of God. Without him, there is no life. With him is the fullness of life, eternal life, abundant life. With Jesus, your life will never be the same. You have embarked upon a journey, an adventure that will take you places you have never dreamed. Just place your hand in his and He will lead the way.

Right now, take out the first memory verse, 1 John 5:11-12. Begin to memorize this verse and its reference. Put the memory verses in your wallet or purse for ready access!

When can you memorize Bible verses? Check the following times when you have 5-10 extra minutes each day.

- ☐ **Before or after breakfast**
- ☐ **Commuting to work**
- ☐ **Lunch break**
- ☐ **Coffee break**
- ☐ **Before or after dinner**
- ☐ **Right before going to bed**

Ask God to help you commit to the process of memorizing Bible verses.

Unit 1, Day 2
God and Man, A Broken Relationship
The Hard Truth

God is *powerful*. We usually don't struggle believing that concept, do we? But did you know that God's power is available to you? From Scripture, we see that God can heal our diseases, control our circumstances, and release us from problems that have troubled us for years. That's good news!

God is *personal*. We often overlook that fact. He loves you, and He wants you to think of Him as your Heavenly Father. You don't have to do *one single thing* to make Him love you more. You are now His child, and He cares for you.

How have you usually pictured God in the past?

- ☐ **Distant and unconcerned**
- ☐ **Harsh and cruel**
- ☐ **Loving and generous**
- ☐ **I didn't believe there was a God**
- ☐ **Other (Specify):** _____

For good or bad, our relationships with earthly fathers shape our view of God and His relationship with us. Even the best earthly fathers cannot fully demonstrate God's character. God's Word helps us to understand God's real nature and His concern for each of us. In John 3:16-17 we read:

> *"For God so loved the world that He gave His one and only Son, that whoever believes in Him shall not perish but have eternal life. For God did not send His Son into the world to condemn the world, but to save the world through Him."*

Based on these verses, how would you describe God?

_____

_____

_____

SIN SEPARATES

Even though God loves us, our sin separates us from Him. Every one of us, without exception, has broken the tie that God made to us when He created Adam and Eve. The results of that separation are devastating. In Romans 3:23 we see that *all* people have sinned and come short of God's glory. In Romans 6:23 we see that the wages of sin is *death*. Without God, the human situation is hopeless. Before you became a Christian, *your* situation was hopeless. Why? Your sin separated you from God!

It would be nice to believe that we possessed a little "spark of goodness" which we could fan into a flame. Unfortunately, that's not true.

Read Isaiah 64:6 to discover how our best efforts look to God.

"All of us have become like one who is unclean, and all our righteous acts are like filthy rags; we all shrivel up like a leaf, and like the wind our sins sweep us away."

What stands out to you about this passage?

_____

_____

You may be wondering how to define sin. Sin is rebellion against God or missing the mark of God's glorious will. You may also be confused about the difference between the word *sin* and the word *sins*. Think of *sin* as a root word, and *sins* as a fruit word.

How have you thought of sin in the past?
- ☐ **All the bad deeds that you have done**
- ☐ **Putting yourself on the throne of your life**
- ☐ **I am not sure**
- ☐ **Other:** _____

Simply stated, sin means putting yourself on the throne of your life. This root sin (putting yourself on the throne of your life) results in the fruit of other sins — evil thoughts, deeds, attitudes, and words. Sin is a condition in which you and I have declared that we are the master — the king — the owner — the boss — of our own lives. That's what makes us unacceptable to God. He never intended for us to own ourselves.

In fact, this total rebellion against God's ownership brings *wrath*. Read the following words from Romans 2:5.

"But because of your stubbornness and your unrepentant heart, you are storing up wrath against yourself for the day of God's wrath, when His righteous judgment will be revealed."

Some people want to avoid this point, saying that God's love cancels out wrath. But if we look at what this verse is saying, we realize that *we* are the ones *storing up wrath for ourselves*. God isn't doing it to *us* we are doing it to *ourselves*!

If a man commits murder, do we accuse the judge of being unreasonable when he declares the criminal guilty? Of course not! The murderer was responsible for his destiny.

You and I are responsible for our destiny. When we realize this, we often try to find a way to patch things up with God. Have you ever thought that doing good works, being religious, or being a good person would make up for your sin? Most people falsely think that these actions will create a way to God. Jesus made the way for us to overcome sin, and He has given this way to you. Jesus made the way to God by sacrificing Himself.

"Jesus answered, 'I am the way and the truth and the life.'"

Unit 1, Day 3
Jesus Made A Way
The Good News

On the previous pages, you learned some distressing news: your sin separates you from God. In fact, there is no way you can approach God yourself. Why? Your best efforts are like filthy rags to Him. But Jesus made a way for you to have a relationship with God. Jesus became like us so that we can enter into the fullness of life with God. That's good news!

JESUS — GOD WITH US

Jesus said, "Anyone who has seen me has seen the Father (God)." Even though we do not see Jesus physically today, we can see him through what is recorded in the Bible. Jesus is both fully God and fully human. Jesus took on earthly flesh and became a man so that he could fully identify with each and every one of us. He understands our joys and pains, our health and sickness, our living and dying.

Visualize this by imagining that God "made his dwelling" among humans. In other words, he "pitched His tent" in our camp. Through this camping out, Jesus provided a way for us to understand God because he adopted our language to show us who He is. As a new believer, you are on an amazing journey. But God made the most amazing journey of all when Jesus came to earth as a man!

Read the following words from John 1:1&14 to gain insight into Jesus' extraordinary journey.

> *"In the beginning was the Word, and the Word was with God, and the Word was God. . . . The Word became flesh and made his dwelling among us. We have seen his glory, the glory of the One and Only, who came from the Father, full of grace and truth."*

What stands out to you from these verses?

_____

_____

JESUS — SAVIOR AND LORD

Because we cannot approach God on our own, because we cannot overcome our sinful state, we need a savior. *Jesus is our Savior!* His amazing love for humanity and His unswerving devotion to the Father's will led Jesus to the cross.

Read Romans 5:8 to see the depth of God's love.

> *"But God demonstrates his love for us in this: While we were still sinners, Christ died for us."*

What feelings do you have as you read this passage?

_____

_____

✖ Thank Jesus for dying for you, for being your Savior!

_____

_____

_____

_____

_____

Yesterday, we read the beginning of John 14:6. Now we will look at the entire verse:

"Jesus answered, 'I am the way and the truth and the life. No one comes to the Father except through me.'"

✖ What does it mean to you that Jesus is the way to God?

_____

_____

_____

Jesus tells us that He is the way to God. Because Jesus gave His life for you, you don't have to wander around in the forest looking for the right path. He is walking beside you, leading you in the way of truth and life.

In order for you to enter into the fullness of this journey, you must realize an important truth. Jesus saved you from a self-owned, self-directed, and self-destructive life. He saved you to show you a better way. The way to know your Savior fully is to give Him the right to be your Lord. When He is Lord of your life, He will lead you down paths that most people only dream about. Your life will be transformed through the experience of His love and His power. It cost Him His life on the cross to provide you with this opportunity. It will cost you the right to control your life as you realize that your Lord can do a better job with your life than you can.

Take time right now to give Jesus the right to be the Savior and Lord of your life. Pray, "Jesus, all I know about myself I give to all I know about You!"

Unit 1, Day 4
God's Guidance
Listening to God

Right now, you are probably thrilled with your relationship with God. You sense His close presence. You know that He speaks to you. You experience His wonderful forgiveness and love. You cannot imagine that you will ever question His direction.

Sadly, many Christians reach a point in their journey where they feel isolated. They wonder why God seems distant and why God's direction seems unclear. But this need not be the case.

GOD WILL ALWAYS BE WITH YOU

In a glorious, mysterious way God resides in you. You may think you will never forget this truth, but even the heroes of faith questioned God's abiding presence.

Read Joshua 1:5; 9 to see how God encouraged Joshua.

> *"No one will be able to stand up against you all the days of your life. As I was with Moses, so I will be with you; I will never leave you nor forsake you. . . . Have I not commanded you? Be strong and courageous. Do not be terrified; do not be discouraged, for the Lord your God will be with you wherever you go."*

According to these verses, what does God promise?

_____

_____

What does God command?

_____

_____

The disciples struggled with God's abiding presence. Sensing the disciples' doubts and fears, Jesus said, "And I will ask the Father, and he will give you another Counselor to be with you forever." (John 14:16) Jesus assured the disciples that, through the Spirit, He would remain with them forever. There may come a time when you doubt God's presence. But remember, God will always be with you. He promised!

How will you respond whenever you feel that God is abandoning you?

- ☐ **Scream**
- ☐ **Doubt**
- ☐ **Remember His promise to be with me always**
- ☐ **Pull away from God**
- ☐ **Remain faithful to Him**

You should have checked 3 and 5.

GOD WILL DIRECT YOU

Jesus promised another, a Counselor to abide with and direct the disciples. God's Spirit directs us too. As you are directed by God's Spirit, you can make godly choices in life. You can know with certainty that your actions will please God. You do not have to make poor choices continually. You do not have to repeat the same mistakes. You can, as one pastor states, "dump dumbbell living!"

> *"But when he, the Spirit of truth, comes, he will guide you into all truth. He will not speak on his own; he will speak only what he hears, and he will tell you what is yet to come." (John 16:13)*

God's Spirit will direct you as you rely on Him.

What are examples of specific ways He directs His followers?

_____

_____

_____

First, God directs his followers through the Bible. Daily Bible reading and weekly Bible verse memorization are important. Why? God speaks through His Word! As you read and memorize the Bible, you will find specific direction for many areas of your life. God will point out areas where you need to grow, areas where you need to repent, areas where He is already at work, transforming your life. Make reading and memorizing God's Word a priority in your spiritual growth!

Second, God directs his followers through prayer. Next week, you will begin to learn about the Listening Room. As you begin to speak to God and listen for His voice, you will know that God directs you to "give-up" ungodly behaviors and "take on" Christ-like actions and attitudes. God speaks through prayer.

Third, God directs his followers through his people, the church. Tomorrow, you will see in greater detail the importance of the church. Know that God speaks through other Christians to direct you, and that He speaks through you to direct other Christians. You need each other!

Continue to memorize 1 John 5:11-12.

Unit 1, Day 5
You Are Not Alone
The Family of God

As you presented your life to Christ, He immediately placed His presence within you! You will never be alone again. But there is another important truth you must know: Jesus has also brought other persons around you and has joined you to them. Together with them, you are the body of Christ, His "called-out ones." You will gather with them in cell groups, building up one another and also revealing His presence to those who do not know Him.

WHAT IS A CELL GROUP?

You probably received this booklet from someone in a "cell group." By joining her or his group, your life will be strengthened by believers who will seek to guide you through the stages of spiritual growth. Apart from this relationship, you will never discover freedom from the power of sin.

A Place for Growth

The Bible describes your present need: ". . . like newborn babies, crave pure spiritual milk, so that by it you may grow up in your salvation." (1 Peter 2:2) Involve yourself immediately in a cell group. Consider those people your spiritual family. You will find more mature believers who will minister to you. More importantly, as you participate in the weekly cell group meetings, you'll observe the way more mature Christians live and serve. They will be good models, or examples for you to observe.

In Titus 2:7 we read Paul's encouragement to a young pastor.

"In everything set them an example by doing what is good."

Think about the people in your cell group. What positive traits do they demonstrate? What can you learn from their example?

_____

_____

_____

A Place for Service

As you grow in your new life, your cell group will be a place where you can relax with fellow believers. The weekly meeting will be a time for sharing joys and problems. In your midst is the Christ who dwells IN you. He's the One who fills the time with His presence and His power. During those gatherings, others will minister to you, <u>and</u> you will minister to others. You will also discover how to use the gifts of the Spirit to build up others and to share your faith with your friends who are not Christians.

WHY IS THE CELL GROUP CRUCIAL TO YOUR NEW LIFE IN CHRIST?

James 5:16 instructs believers to confess sins to each other and pray for each other so that they may be healed. By becoming responsible and accountable to others in the

12

body of Christ we participate with God in breaking the power of sin in our lives. Confessing our sins unlocks the deep issues of our heart, and humility holds the door open so genuine transformation can occur.

In the cell group, pride and sin are stripped of their power. You will quickly discover that you are strengthened by the group's encouragement, and the group is strengthened by your encouragement. Thus, you will grow both by helping and by being helped. By sharing with Christians we know well, we discover how to overcome the power of sin in our lives. It cannot be done in isolation from the body of Christ!

Below, you will find a covenant. Please read it and examine your heart as you consider signing it. Share your commitment with your cell group leader. Living according to this covenant will bring a freeing and exciting life to each step you take.

My Personal Covenant

Knowing that Christ has brought me His peace, I will declare
Him to be Lord over all my life.
My body, my possessions, and my future are His to command.
I will join my life to a Cell Group and consider it my
Basic Christian Community.
I will respond to all with God's acceptance. I will not be judgmental.
I will always remember that God allows all things for
His eternal purposes.
I will learn to pray and seek to know how to hear His voice speaking
to me. I will prayerfully seek to know what, in
each situation, God wants to address, and be His
instrument of healing.
Knowing that my Cell Group may be a turning point for my life
or that of another person, I covenant to place my
commitment to its ministry at the very
top of my priority list.
As God anoints me, I shall be His instrument to save, to heal,
to deliver, and to restore others.
In this spirit, I invite His Spirit to take my life and use it
for His glory.

Name: _____   Date: _____

Unit 2, Day 1
How To Listen To Your Lord
The Listening Room

YOUR GOAL: DEVELOP A RELATIONSHIP, NOT A RELIGION!

"To all who received him (Christ), to those who believed in his name, he gave the right to become children of God" (John 1:12).

🌹 **Based on the verse above, how does someone become a child of God?**

☐   **By religious pursuits**

☐   **By receiving Jesus Christ**

☐   **I am not sure**

Did you check the second answer above? Is it becoming clear to you that when you accepted Christ as your Savior, you didn't receive a *religion*, you received a *Person* — the living Christ — into your life. Christianity isn't primarily a system of laws and beliefs. It is first and foremost a personal relationship with a loving God who wants to commune with you and guide you through life's journey. Like any growing relationship, this fellowship is two-way. God wants to listen to your concerns and your words of praise and thanks to Him, but He also wants to speak to you — to guide you and encourage you.

Jesus' desire for close fellowship with you is expressed in His words:

"Here I am! I stand at the door and knock. If anyone hears my voice and opens the door, I will come in and eat with him, and he with me" (Revelation 3:20).

🌹 **What impresses you most about Jesus' words to you in this verse?**

_____

_____

THE LISTENING ROOM

A servant functions only after he or she receives the master's orders. As you learn to listen to God's voice, you will find direction in fulfilling His will. Some think God does not communicate directly with us. That is not true! He speaks to us. We must learn to listen.

To hear God effectively, you need to include a Listening Room in your lifestyle. The image comes from an encounter between an American pastor and a Japanese pastor. While hosting the American pastor, the Japanese pastor took his new friend outside for a tour of the family garden. A one-room cottage stood in a corner of the garden. When the American pastor inquired about its purpose, his host explained that the cottage was his Listening Room, a special place where he spent time to hear God's voice.

The Listening Room is more a *condition of the heart* than a physical place. It means opening our lives not only to speak to Him, but also to hear from Him. The prophet Habakkuk displayed this attitude when he wrote:

"I will stand at my watch . . . I will look to see what he will say to me. . . .
Then the Lord replied, 'Write down' the revelation . . . " (Habakkuk 2:1-2).

Since God speaks to us, the question for us is not, *"Is God speaking?"* The right question is, *"Am I listening?"*

HOW HAS GOD ALREADY SPOKEN TO YOU?

Think about this: the fact that you are a Christian is proof that God does speak, that you do hear Him and that you know how to respond to Him!

You are a Christian because you have heard the voice of God calling you. Therefore, nothing in this lesson is new to you! You have heard His voice at least once, perhaps many more times.

Where were you when God spoke to you about accepting Jesus as your Savior and Lord?

_____

_____

Was His call to you a single, powerful word from Him or was it a growing sense of His call to you to receive Him?

_____

How did you respond? Did you share what you were sensing or experiencing with a friend, cell leader or pastor? If so, write the name(s) below:

_____

LISTEN TO HIS VOICE!

"Jesus said, 'If anyone has ears to hear, let him hear'" (Mark 4:23).

Spend time now in the Listening Room. You don't have to seek Him — *He is seeking you!* God is creating spiritual ears in you to listen to Him. The starting point is not your desire for Him, but His desire for you. Your longing for Him springs from His longing for you.

You may wish to begin your listening time with this simple prayer: "Lord Jesus, I thank You for loving me and calling me to Yourself. I give all that I know about me to all that I know about You!" Then be silent and listen for His voice.

Did you sense God speaking to you? Jot below impressions you sensed to be His voice:

_____

_____

This week, memorize 1 Corinthians 10:13, your second Scripture verse.

Unit 2, Day 2
How To Listen To Your Lord
Christ is in You!

WHERE IS CHRIST WHEN HE COMMUNES WITH YOU?

When you hear Christ speaking, He is not speaking from heaven, from somewhere far away. *He is speaking from within you.* The Apostle Paul said that this was the "great secret" or "mystery" of the Christian message: *"Christ in you, the hope of glory" (Colossians 1:27).* Jesus has taken up residence in your heart!

God doesn't live in a building. He lives in you! When you commune with Christ, He is in your inner being.

> *"I pray that out of his glorious riches he may strengthen you with power through his Spirit in your inner being" (Ephesians 3:16).*

According to this verse, where is God's strengthening Spirit at work?

_____

_____

_____

Because Christ's Spirit is always with you in your inner being, you can talk to Him at anytime!

WHICH PART OF YOU COMMUNES WITH GOD?

This diagram helps explain your communion with God and how it impacts your life.

God the *Father, Son and Holy Spirit* dwells in your inner being, but His fellowship with you touches all of your life — body, spirit, mind, will and emotions. If you present yourself completely to Him, He will have the right to work in every part of your life. He can touch your *body* to bring healing. He may touch your *mind* to set you free from doubt. He can minister to your *emotions* to set you free from fear, guilt and low self-esteem. He will touch your *will* and you will know His guidance! God wants His power to flow through *every part of you* — your thoughts, desires, emotions and decisions. As you commune with Him, you'll see Him do His beautiful work in every part of your being.

16

You may wonder what the "strongholds" are in the diagram. They are areas of your life which have not yet come fully under the Lordship of Christ. You may be struggling to overcome some of them. You may not even be aware of others. They don't belong in your life, and God will be removing them as you hear His voice and quietly yield them to Him. You'll learn more next week about how God brings you freedom from strongholds.

HOW TO LISTEN TO CHRIST WITHIN

Here are some practical suggestions to guide you as you learn to listen to the voice of Christ within:

1. *Be completely open to God.* Don't avoid areas that you don't want Him to tamper with. Let him speak His direction into every area of your life. Often taking this step immediately causes you to hear His voice.

2. *Realize that at the first signal from us, God runs to greet us.* Jesus says in Revelation 3:20:

> "Here I am! I stand at the door and knock. If anyone hears my voice and opens the door, I will come in and eat with him, and he with me."

He desires to joyfully welcome us into His presence and to embrace us in His warm acceptance.

3. *You can begin your listening time with a simple prayer.* This is what the prophet Samuel prayed when he was still a child:

> "Speak, Lord, for your servant is listening" (1 Samuel 3:10).

4. *Wait quietly for His promptings.* Don't get impatient. Sometimes His Word comes immediately. At other times, God waits for us to enter into a greater silence before speaking so that He has our full attention.

Come to God now in prayer, yielding yourself to Him with the words of Samuel and listening for His voice as he did.

✎ **What do you hear or sense? Is He leading you to meditate on a certain Scripture? Is He impressing you to pray for or to serve a certain person? Is He speaking to you about a certain relationship or problem in your life? Listen! Listen! Record your impressions below:**

_____

_____

_____

_____

This week, continue to memorize 1 Corinthians 10:13, your second Scripture verse, and review 1 John 5:11-12.

Unit 2, Day 3
How To Listen To Your Lord
Using Scripture in the Listening Room

RECOGNIZING A FAMILIAR VOICE

When my earthly father calls me on the telephone, I immediately know who it is. I instantly recognize his voice because I have heard it for many years. If a new acquaintance calls, however, it's different. I can't identify the caller easily because I haven't spent much time listening to him.

As you learn to listen to your heavenly Father, your ability to hear and discern His voice will grow. One of the most helpful ways for you to learn to recognize His voice is by reading and memorizing Scripture. As you listen to His voice come to you through Scripture, you'll be able to hear that same voice as His Spirit speaks special direction and encouragement for your own life. The same Spirit who inspired the Bible speaks to you in the Listening Room.

When you study and memorize Scripture, it will do more than build your faith and renew your mind: it will also heighten your sensitivity to God's voice.

THE BIBLE — GOD'S INSPIRED WORD

The Bible is God's Word, inspired by His Spirit.

"All Scripture is God-breathed . . ." (2 Timothy 3:16).

"Above all else, you must understand that no prophecy of Scripture came about by the prophet's own interpretation. For prophecy never had its origin in the will of man, but men spoke from God as they were carried along by the Holy Spirit" (2 Peter 1:20-21)

 According to these passages, what is the origin of Scripture?

_____

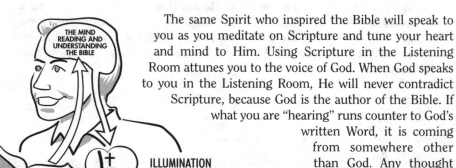

The same Spirit who inspired the Bible will speak to you as you meditate on Scripture and tune your heart and mind to Him. Using Scripture in the Listening Room attunes you to the voice of God. When God speaks to you in the Listening Room, He will never contradict Scripture, because God is the author of the Bible. If what you are "hearing" runs counter to God's written Word, it is coming from somewhere other than God. Any thought not consistent with the teaching of Scripture is to be instantly rejected.

ILLUMINATION
As I direct my heart and mind to seek the Lord, His Spirit speaks into my heart, impressing His thoughts and ideas directly upon it.

18

When a believer is listening for God's voice and "hears" something that runs counter to the teaching of Scripture, what do you think its source of origin might be? (Check all that apply.)

☐   Thoughts from his or her own mind.

☐   Mixed motives in their heart that wants to pull them in different directions.

☐   Voices from the past that are out of tune with God's word.

☐   Satan.

☐   All of the above.

The correct answer is "all of the above." Thoughts from our minds may temporarily confuse us. At other times, our hearts may not be pure, so we try to "hear" what we want to hear. Misleading voices from our past also pop into our minds or Satan may try to mislead us. How can we tell the origin of thoughts? By tuning our listening with Scripture.

Piano tuners often use a tuning fork when they tune a piano's strings. The tuning fork has a pitch that stays true and unchanging. They can't tune the piano by simply listening to its own strings. If they did, it would slowly get far out of tune. They need an external, unchanging standard. When they strike the tuning fork and listen carefully to its unalterable pitch, they can then perfectly align the piano's tune.

The Bible, God's Word, plays a similar role in our lives. It offers the unchanging standard that attunes our spirits, hearts and minds to hear God's voice.

MEDITATING ON GOD'S WORD

Find the book of 1 John in your Bible. (It is very close to the end of your Bible, just a few pages in front of the last book, Revelation.) 1 John was a letter sent to early Christians by Jesus' follower, the Apostle John. Say a short prayer inviting God to speak to you through His Word; then read the first chapter of 1 John.

What stands out to you from this chapter? Does God seem to be emphasizing a certain truth to you?

_____

Ask God if there are other things that He wants to speak to you. Make notes below.

_____

_____

_____

Continue to work on memorizing 1 Corinthians 10:13.

Unit 2, Day 4
How To Listen To Your Lord
Learning to Hear God's Voice

JESUS — THE LIVING WAY

As important as the Bible is for helping you hear God's voice, it isn't enough in itself. In fact, some people have studied the Bible for years and years and *still* have missed God's life and purpose. Jesus spoke to first century religious scholars like this in John 5:39-40:

> *"You diligently study the Scriptures because you think that by them you possess eternal life. These are the Scriptures that testify about me, yet you refuse to come to me to have life."*

The center of our faith is not the Bible, but Jesus. The Bible is written to point us to Him! Psalms 119:105 says:

> *"Your word is a lamp to my feet and a light for my path."*

God's Word lights our path. It's like the headlights of a car on a highway at night. It *lights* the way, but *isn't* the way. Jesus says in John 14:6:

> *"I am the way and the truth and the life. No one comes to the Father except through me."*

Jesus is the only way to the Father!

 What other ways have you tried? What were the results?

_____

A SPECIAL HELPER

To help us deepen our relationship with Him, Jesus gives us a very special Helper, the Holy Spirit. Read the promises below that Jesus gave His followers before His death:

> *"I will ask the Father, and he will give you another Counselor, to be with you forever, the Spirit of truth . . . you know him, for he lives with you and will be in you. I will not leave you as orphans; I will come to you" (John 14:16-18).*

> *"I tell you the truth: It is for your good that I am going away. Unless I go away, the Counselor will not come to you; but if I go, I will send him to you" (John 16:7).*

> *"I have much more to say to you, more than you can now bear. But when he, the Spirit of truth, comes he will guide you into all truth. He will bring glory to me by taking from what is mine and making it known to you" (John 16:14).*

Based on these promises, what do we know about the work of God's spirit? (Check all the statements that follow which are true.)

- [ ] **The Holy Spirit is a counselor (special companion) to us**
- [ ] **Jesus continues to guide us today by the voice of His Spirit**
- [ ] **The Spirit's job is to bring glory to Jesus**
- [ ] **Having The Holy Spirit's presence is almost as good as having Jesus Himself physically present with us**

Did you check all of the answers above as correct? If so, you were almost completely right. You should have checked all of them except the last one. In John 16:7, Jesus says that the presence of His Spirit is even better than His physical presence! Why? Verse 14 gives us the clue: He is not only *with* us, He is also *in* us! When Christ speaks to you, it is not a long distance call from a remote part of the universe. It is from *within* as your constant Companion and Counselor.

LISTENING TO THE SPIRIT

Hearing the voice of God's Spirit often requires us to listen in a new and deeper way. In the past, your thoughts simply flowed from your mind. Thoughts from the Spirit, however, don't originate in your own thought processes. They come from God's Spirit in your "inner being."

That is not to say that we are to be "mindless." God renews and uses our minds. Yet part of learning to hear God involves quieting the whirl of our thoughts so that we can sense the inner promptings of the Spirit.

✎ **Answer these true/false questions to help you see to what extent you have been unaware of the spiritual realm and have relied only on your mind:**

T F

- [ ] [ ] **In the past, true reality for me has been in the physical world alone, not in the physical and the spiritual realms.**
- [ ] [ ] **I have calculated, analytical thoughts, rather than letting the Spirit place flowing thoughts in my mind.**
- [ ] [ ] **I base my decisions solely on my own wisdom, rather than waiting on God for his thoughts, burdens and visions.**
- [ ] [ ] **I interact with the Bible on only a mental level, rather than letting God impress special truths upon me by His Spirit.**

How can you distinguish the promptings of God's Spirit from your own thoughts? Here are some practical tips:

1. Thoughts from your mind are meditated. But thoughts spoken by Christ's Spirit to your spirit are spontaneous ideas, words, feelings or images.
2. You sense the thoughts coming from your heart, not from your mind.
3. The Spirit's thoughts will sometimes have an unusual content to them. They will bring ideas, insights or instructions that you wouldn't have thought of yourself.
4. They will bring with them a sense of peace and spiritual power.
5. When you act on the Spirit's promptings, they will bring joy and freedom.

Remember — even though God speaks, it is up to you to turn your attention to Him and listen for His voice.

Unit 2, Day 5
How To Listen To Your Lord
Your Own Listening Room

A SPECIAL TIME, A SPECIAL PLACE

The Japanese pastor mentioned on page 14 had a little cottage that served as a Listening Room. Not all of us can build a special room for just this purpose, but we can all create a special time in our schedule and have a quiet place in our home.

It looks like Jesus had such a Listening Room. When He was in the vicinity of Jerusalem, He used the Mount of Olives, which lay east of the city, as a special place to retreat and pray. The Gospel of Luke tells us that He went there each evening (Luke 21:37). It was in that garden He prayed into the night, pouring out His Heart to the Father to receive strength and resolve to go to the cross for us.

As He crisscrossed the land of Israel, He found other such Listening Rooms. Luke 5:16 reports: *"Jesus often withdrew to lonely places and prayed."*

Six centuries before Christ, the Prophet Daniel also had a Listening Room. Three times each day he met with God in *"his upstairs room where the windows opened toward Jerusalem"* (Daniel 6:10).

You may be thinking, "Why do I need a special time and place? Can't I talk to God and hear His voice throughout the day?"

It's true that you can and should commune with Christ throughout your day. At the same time, you need to realize that if you take a special time to tune in and focus on Him, you will be more sensitive to His words of love, challenge and encouragement throughout the scurry of your activity.

Devoting time and effort to any relationship is required for love to grow. Your relationship with God is no different.

HOW TO CREATE YOUR OWN LISTENING ROOM

Perhaps you have already begun to establish a special time and place to meet your Lord. If so, great! Whether you already have a special daily time or are just beginning, here are some things to consider in "building" your own Listening Room.

🌹 **What could be a special time and place in your daily schedule for you to read, pray and listen to God?**

Time: _____

Place: _____

Are you a "night person" or a "morning person?" You may need to experiment to discover the best time and place to add this new habit to your life. If at first you don't succeed, try a different location or time. Ask God for His wisdom and insight. He eagerly wants to meet with you!

🖊️ **What changes will you need to make in your schedule to allow for this time? (For example, you may need to get up earlier if you plan to make time in the morning. If you plan to take time in the evening, you may need to rearrange appointments or your TV viewing habits.)**

_____

_____

If you had a personal appointment with the leader of your country, you wouldn't let anything interrupt your schedule. In your Listening Room you are meeting with the Creator of the Universe. What an awesome privilege and opportunity! Nothing could be more important.

🖊️ **What might interrupt your time with God? How could you eliminate or minimize these various interruptions?**

_____

_____

To minimize interruptions, it's helpful to talk with family members or roommates to let them know you will be taking time with God and you don't want to be disturbed except for emergencies. (Maybe you can also help make uninterrupted time available for them.)

DRAW NEAR WITH ANTICIPATION AND EXPECTANCY
Over and over in the Bible there is an appeal to approach God to experience His life and joy:

> *"Come, all you who are thirsty, come to the waters; and you who have no money, come, buy and eat! Come, buy wine and milk without money and without cost. Why spend money on what is not bread, and your labor on what does not satisfy? Listen, listen to me, and eat what is good, and your soul will delight in the richest of fare"* (Isaiah 55:1-2).

> *"If anyone is thirsty, let him come to me and drink. Whoever believes in me, as the Scripture has said, streams of living water will flow from within him"* (John 7:39).

🖊️ **Circle the word "come" in the passages above.**

🖊️ **What does God promise to do as you continue to approach Him?**

_____

_____

Christ is calling you and has wonderful things to share with you. Don't think of your time with Him as an obligation, but as a joyful, divine appointment — a special time set aside and anticipated by both of you.

Unit 3, Day 1
Receive Christ's Freedom
Freedom From Guilt

"So if the Son sets you free, you will be free indeed" (John 8:36).

The Christian life is a life of freedom. Satan desires to place people in bondage to sin, fear, and deception. But Jesus died to set us free from every one of these bondages. This week, you'll be learning how to gain Jesus' freedom in every area of your life.

DO YOU KNOW YOUR SINS HAVE BEEN FORGIVEN?

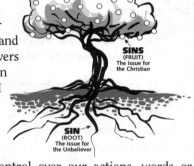

Do you remember the definition of "sin?" Sin is putting *yourself* on the throne of your life, rather than Christ. It means rejecting God and His plans and going your own way. Sin is the issue which unbelievers come face to face with when considering salvation and the claims of Christ. They must ask, "Am I willing to turn from self to Christ and receive the cleansing and freedom that He offers?"

As Christians, the issue for us is *"sins,"* not *"sin."* Although we have chosen to follow Christ, we still occasionally disobey and reject God's control over our actions, words or attitudes. When we do, God offers us a wonderful promise:

"If we confess our sins, he is faithful and just and will forgive us our sins and purify us from all unrighteousness" (1 John 1:9).

 Based on this verse, what must you do to be forgiven and cleansed?

_____

The word confess means to "agree with God." It means we admit we have sinned, rather than denying it or making excuses.

Notice the extent of God's forgiveness in 1 John 1:9. He cleanses us from all unrighteousness! Psalms 103:12 tells us how far these sins are removed:

"As far as the east is from the west, so far has he removed our transgressions from us."

God's forgiveness is complete! You needn't wonder if God forgives you when you confess your sins; He faithfully and fully forgives and cleanses you.

DAVID: AN EXAMPLE OF GOD'S FORGIVENESS

King David was guilty of serious sin, including lust, adultery, treachery and murder. Yet he confessed his sin to God in Psalms 51:4:

"Against you, you only, have I sinned and done what is evil in your sight, so that you are proved right when you speak and justified when you judge."

When David confessed in 2 Samuel 12:13, *"I have sinned against the Lord!"* God's prophet, Nathan, instantly said, *"The Lord has taken away your sin."*

GOD FORGIVES YOU!

It shouldn't surprise you that God generously forgives you, since that is the very reason that He sent Jesus to die for you.

"This is love: not that we loved God, but that he loved us and sent his Son as an atoning sacrifice for our sins" (1 John 4:10).

According to this verse, why don't you need to fear God's punishment when you confess your sin?

_____

_____

Isn't it wonderful to know that Jesus has taken your punishment? When you admit you were wrong, that you took back the control of your life and rejected His Lordship, God hears your confession and declares: *"You are already forgiven!"* Spend some time in the Listening Room right now. Ask God to search your heart and to reveal any unconfessed sins in your life. Then bring those sins to God, specifically confessing them to Him. Pray:

"Father, I confess (a specific attitude or action) as my sin, I turn from it and I ask you to forgive me."

Once you have prayed, remember that you have no right to live with guilt about what He has forgiven! Do not allow yourself to ever think, "Well, God has forgiven me because He is God. I am grateful that He has done so, but it does not mean I can forgive *myself!* I do not feel I deserve to be forgiven by *me*, so I am going to continue to punish myself. I am still bad even though God has forgiven me." This is a subtle denial of the power of God and causes you to become supreme to Him in your self-judgment which you place above His forgiveness.

Thoughtfully write a prayer in the space below, thanking Him for His forgiveness and cleansing:

_____

_____

_____

_____

_____

Memorize 1 John 1:9 this week.

Unit 3, Day 2
Receive Christ's Freedom
What is a "Stronghold?"

STRONGHOLDS DEFINED:

You may recall that we have already learned that *strongholds* are areas of our lives that have not come fully under the lordship of Jesus (refer to the diagram on page 16).

Do you know where the word *"strongholds"* originates? It was first used in the Old Testament. When the nation of Israel conquered the Promised Land, they displaced peoples and nations more powerful than themselves. God told the nation of Israel to utterly destroy all of the people who had previously inhabited the land. This may sound harsh, but the tribes that lived there had performed vile rituals, including infant sacrifices, for centuries. Unfortunately, the leaders of Israel disobeyed Jehovah's orders. Although they conquered many powerful and well-defended cities, they left some heavily fortified places. These areas were called *strongholds*. These *strongholds* were *pockets of resistance* — areas they allowed to remain. Some of these *strongholds* were well-defended cities. The city of Jerusalem, for example, remained out of Israel's control for several hundred years. In other cases, the *strongholds* were small desert hideouts for small bands of marauders. In every case, the *strongholds* caused endless misery, bloodshed, and heartache, eventually bringing Israel to defeat.

In the New Testament, *stronghold* is used to refer to areas in our lives not fully under Christ's control. For example, in 2 Corinthians 10:4-5, Paul writes:

> *"The weapons we fight with are not the weapons of the world. On the contrary, they have divine power to demolish strongholds. We demolish arguments and every pretension that sets itself up against the knowledge of God, and we take captive every thought to make it obedient to Christ."*

Based on these verses, which of the following statements would you say are true?

☐   **We are engaged in a spiritual battle.**

☐   **We battle evil the same way unbelievers do.**

☐   **We have powerful weapons to win our battles.**

☐   **Our goal is to have every thought and attitude in tune with our relationship with God.**

☐   **Strongholds are often in our minds.**

(You should have checked all answers except the second one.)

Like the people of Israel, we are engaged in warfare, but we are not fighting with our will power and personal resources only. We use powerful God-given weapons, like the truth of His Word and insights provided by His Spirit. His weapons have the power to set people free and bring them fully under Christ's lordship.

WHAT DOES A STRONGHOLD LOOK LIKE?

When we receive Christ and surrender our lives to Him, there are almost always areas not yet completely controlled by Him. Although we sincerely seek to follow Christ with all our hearts, there are hurts, habits or long-standing attitudes that still need Christ's healing and freedom. Sometimes the strongholds are tiny pockets of resistance. At other times they are long-standing fortified areas.

For example, a young father accepted Christ. He was a sincere Christian with real leadership potential. However, he would "fly off the handle" in anger toward family members. When he asked some Christian brothers to pray for him, God's Spirit revealed a stronghold in his life: pornography. This had allowed Satan an entry into his life. As is sometimes the case, this oppression manifested itself in the seemingly unrelated area of anger. When he confessed this sin and destroyed his magazines, God delivered him from his rage, and he began a journey of walking out his deliverance by God's grace.

One of Sue's strongholds was more subtle. Instead of listening to Christ's voice and letting Him control her attitudes and actions, she often let fear of rejection direct her life. She was always looking for approval. For her, freedom came as she learned to accept Christ's unconditional acceptance and love and to hear His voice above all others.

As you grow in Christ, you will probably discover sins and habits you have allowed in your life for many years. These might include bitterness and anger toward someone who hurt you, occult practices (horoscopes, fortune telling, idol worship, etc.), habits which destroy your health, addictions, fears or shame from traumatic life experiences, masturbation, pornography, or other lustful habits.

THE VICTORY IS YOURS!

Even after World War 2 ended, pockets of Japanese troops continued to fight viciously. That's similar to what goes on in a Christian's life. The war is over, we have definitely surrendered to Christ and there's no question about the final outcome. But pockets of resistance remain that must be captured.

> "But thanks be to God! He gives us the victory through our Lord Jesus Christ" (1 Corinthians 15:57).

As you examine your life to see where strongholds exist, realize that victory isn't ultimately dependent upon you, but upon what Jesus did for you on the cross. Victory and healing are already yours!

Memorize 1 John 1:9 this week.

Unit 3, Day 3
Receive Christ's Freedom
Freedom from Resentment

BONDAGE OR FREEDOM?

Jesus declared:

> *"The thief (Satan) comes only to steal and kill and destroy; I have come that they may have life, and have it to the full" (John 10:10).*

Christ wants to give abundant life; Satan desires to destroy it. One tool Satan uses to keep people in bondage is *resentment*. Resentment means we hold grudges and refuse to forgive those who have wronged us.

All of us are hurt and offended by others as we go through life. When others wrong us, we can choose to harbor bitterness against them or we can choose to forgive as Christ has forgiven us.

Resentment blocks the flow of God's peace and joy in our lives. It causes bitterness and anger to grow in our hearts. It controls our attitudes and actions by making us react to people and situations out of past hurts rather than with freedom and love. Resentment also becomes a fertile ground where other ailments can grow. Besides poisoning us emotionally, doctors tell us that over time resentment can cause physical problems like back pain, ulcers, arthritis, and high blood pressure.

Sometimes people think that they are punishing someone else by refusing to forgive them. But in reality, the one who suffers most is the one who fails to forgive.

Dr. Timothy Warner, who teaches on freedom in Christ, illustrates it this way. When someone wrongs someone else, there is often a "chain" of resentment formed from the offended to the offender. Time and distance often do nothing to remove the hurt. The offended person(s) is the only one who can remove the hurt. When the offended person(s) chooses to forgive and release the offender(s), the offended person(s) discovers freedom.

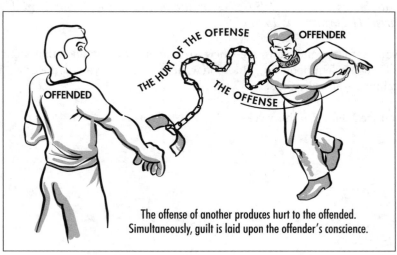

The offense of another produces hurt to the offended.
Simultaneously, guilt is laid upon the offender's conscience.

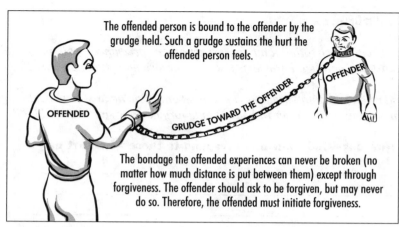

The offended person is bound to the offender by the grudge held. Such a grudge sustains the hurt the offended person feels.

The bondage the offended experiences can never be broken (no matter how much distance is put between them) except through forgiveness. The offender should ask to be forgiven, but may never do so. Therefore, the offended must initiate forgiveness.

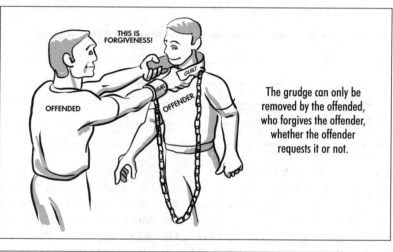

The grudge can only be removed by the offended, who forgives the offender, whether the offender requests it or not.

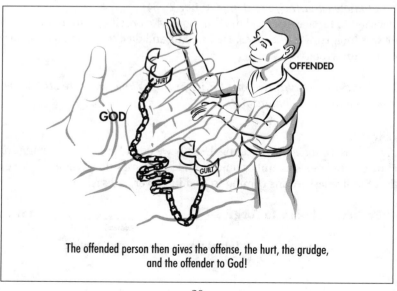

The offended person then gives the offense, the hurt, the grudge, and the offender to God!

THE CALL TO FORGIVE

"Bear with each other and forgive whatever grievances you may have against one another. Forgive as the Lord forgave you" (Colossians 3:13).

"And when you stand praying, if you hold anything against anyone, forgive him, so that your Father in heaven may forgive your sins" (Mark 11:25).

How does God want us to respond to those who hurt us?

_____

_____

_____

_____

In these verses, what and who does Jesus say to forgive?

_____

_____

_____

_____

_____

FORGIVE AS YOU HAVE BEEN FORGIVEN

You might decide to forgive because you want to be whole, free from bitterness and anger. You might choose forgiveness because it is God's command. However, the best reason to forgive is because *Christ forgives you*. When He hung from the cross, His wounds bleeding, His body wracked with pain, He called out, *"Father, forgive them, for they do not know what they are doing"* (Luke 23:34).

His decision to forgive extended beyond those who crucified Him to include you and me. Our sins took Him to the cross. He loved us and died for us in spite of our sin. As the Apostle Paul wrote,

"But God demonstrates his love for us in this: While we were still sinners, Christ died for us" (Romans 5:8).

FORGIVENESS IS . . .

Forgiveness is a *choice*, not a feeling. Usually we don't "feel" like forgiving someone. The feeling comes later, sometimes quickly and sometimes slowly, after we have chosen to forgive. Forgiveness means coming to God in prayer and saying,

"Father, I choose to forgive _____ for . . . ."
                                                    (name)

Using the next page, spend intentional time thinking and praying:

Whom do you need to forgive? Write their names below. Then, write "in the name of Jesus, I forgive you!" after each one:

Parents (living or dead):

_____

_____

Other family members:

_____

_____

_____

_____

Co-workers:

_____

_____

Friends:

_____

_____

Cell Group members:

_____

_____

Others in your past:

_____

_____

Yourself (why?):

_____

_____

Let God gently speak to your heart, bringing people or situations to mind for you to forgive. Some may come to your mind now, others over the course of the week. Whenever it is, come to God in prayer and say, "Father, I forgive . . . ."

If you need His help to forgive, ask Him for it. Your mentor also stands ready to pray with you.

Review all your Scripture verses from previous weeks plus this week.

Unit 3, Day 4
Receive Christ's Freedom
Free from Strongholds

WHO ARE WE FIGHTING?

"For our struggle is not against flesh and blood, but against the rulers, against the authorities, against the powers of this dark world and against the spiritual forces of evil in the heavenly realms" (Ephesians 6:12).

 According to the verse above, whom are we fighting?

_____

We are involved in a war. Satan doesn't want us to experience Christ's abundant life, so we are battling spiritual forces of darkness that want us in bondage. As you learn to defeat these enemies, your faith in God's power will grow and you will be able to minister His freedom to others. Begin now!

DISCERN THE STRONGHOLDS

Some strongholds are easily overcome. Others require a battle. The support and prayer of others is often helpful. Feel free to ask your cell group leader for help. He or she is ready to minister to you or to link you with someone who is especially trained for ministry in this area.

Whether you are praying by yourself or with Christian friends, follow these steps to receive freedom from strongholds in your life. To claim Christ's freedom from strongholds, it's often necessary to have some uninterrupted blocks of time to pray and let God speak to you.

1. *Claim Christ's victory and protection.* Read 1 Corinthians 15:57. Pray, "God, I thank You that You have already paid the full price and that complete victory is mine because Jesus died for me and rose again. As I battle with the enemy and take Your victory, I claim Your full protection over me and my family through the name of Jesus."

2. *Receive God's cleansing.* Read 1 John 1:9 and confess any and all known sins that are not rooted in strongholds in your life.

3. *Surrender to God's will in place of your own.* Tell Him that you want His wholeness and freedom. Invite His Holy Spirit to direct your thoughts. Don't go before Him with your plans; instead, be prepared for Him to show you His plans as He brings to mind specific areas in your life and points the path to freedom.

4. *Confess sins as God brings them to your mind.* Wherever there is a stronghold, there has been an entry point, a sin or experience that gave the enemy an opportunity to put a stronghold into you. Search your heart. Let the Holy Spirit bring possible strongholds to mind. These may include:

Occult involvement. The Bible repeatedly condemns all forms of witchcraft, spiritism and ancestor worship. Have you had your fortune told, used a Ouija board, been involved in false religions or sought any source of spiritual power apart from Jesus Christ? What actions or situations is God's Spirit bringing to your mind? Specifically confess your involvement in each of these things as sin, receiving God's forgiveness.

Anger. The effects of an uncontrolled temper can be devastating. God intends for His followers to demonstrate peaceful love rather than violent hate. Do you have difficulty with violent outbursts? Do you have bitter feelings toward a particular group of people?

Addiction. People wrestle with addictions in many forms: alcohol, drugs, sex, and pornography. Regardless of the addiction, the stronghold is real. Do you struggle with any of the addictions listed above? Do you break-free from the addiction only to return days or even hours later? Confess your addiction and seek God's full cleansing and release.

Resentment. Who has deeply hurt you in the past? Who do you need to forgive? Remember, you don't have to feel like it to choose to forgive. Do you need to forgive any of these: family members, friends or yourself?

DEMOLISH THE STRONGHOLDS!

Paul said that God's weapons, His Word and His Spirit, "demolish strongholds" (2 Corinthians 10:4). When the strongholds are destroyed, Satan no longer has these bases from which to operate in your life. As God highlights specific areas and you confess sin and forgive others, you can then participate with God in demolishing strongholds. You might pray like this:

> "Lord Jesus, I thank You that through Your power I can pull down and destroy all strongholds in my life in the areas of (name areas that you know are creating problems in your life).

> "Wicked spirits, I forbid you to work in these areas again or for any other wicked one to take your place. I declare all your works destroyed in the name of Jesus.

> "In the power and authority of the Lord Jesus Christ, I bind and command you to depart from me. I will consider all your thoughts destroyed and will not allow you to give any false assistance, comfort or reasoning contrary to the Word of God to me. Amen."

 Declare Christ's victory!

Read aloud the Scripture and prayer below:

> "They overcame him by the blood of the Lamb and by the word of their testimony; they did not love their lives so much as to shrink from death" (Revelation 12:11).

> "As your child, O God, I declare that You have overcome and defeated Satan. I overcome the enemy by the blood of the Lamb, the word of my testimony, and a total surrender of my life. I now ask You for a fresh empowering of Your Spirit in every area of my life."

> "Thank You, Lord, for dying for me and for guiding me in receiving Your freedom. In the blessed name of Jesus Christ my Lord. Amen."

As you think about the area of strongholds, what questions do you have that you would like to ask your mentor or cell group leader?

Unit 3, Day 5
Receive Christ's Freedom
Walk in Daily Victory

A SOLDIER WITHOUT A GUN?

Can you imagine a soldier going into battle without his equipment? How effective would he be without a helmet, gun, or ammunition? Not only would this soldier be in a ridiculous and dangerous position, he would even hinder his own army.

The Apostle Paul wrote:

"Our struggle is not against flesh and blood, but against . . . the powers of this dark world . . . Therefore put on the full armor of God, so that when the day of evil comes, you may be able to stand your ground, and after you have done everything, to stand. Stand firm then, with the belt of truth buckled around your waist, with the breastplate of righteousness in place, and with your feet fitted with the readiness that comes from the gospel of peace. In addition to all this, take up the shield of faith, with which you can extinguish all the flaming arrows of the evil one. Take the helmet of salvation and the sword of the Spirit, which is the word of God" (Ephesians 6:12-17).

 Look closely at Ephesians 6:12-17. Draw lines to connect the pieces of armor in the left column to the proper descriptive words in the right column:

Breastplate	Salvation
Footwear	God's Word
Helmet	Truth
Sword	Gospel of Peace
Shield	Righteousness
Belt	Faith

BEGIN EACH DAY EQUIPPED THROUGH PRAYER

Just as you go through the routine of dressing each morning, like a soldier you should begin each day prepared for the battle. What good is it to put on the armor once the battle is over!

Having a prayer time every morning may not be easy at first. In fact, it may be impossible without the Holy Spirit empowering you. Ask God to give you the desire and strength to change a lifetime of habits and to start each day by talking to Him.

Besides thanking God for a new day to serve Him and pouring out your requests to Him, take time to equip yourself for the spiritual battles of your day. Pray something like this:

"Heavenly Father, thank You that You will go with me through this day, that You will bless me and use me to bless others. Today I take Your armor: the belt of truth around me, Your righteousness as a breastplate to guard the desires of my heart, the shoes of the good news of Your peace, the shield of faith to repel the attacks of the evil one, the helmet of salvation to guard the thoughts of my mind, and the sword of the Spirit which is Your Word. I ask You to surround each member of my family with Your protection as they walk through this day. Guard them from physical and spiritual harm. I believe You to do this and I thank You for it!"

POWER TO OVERCOME

God doesn't expect you to live your life in your own power. He offers you the empowering of His Spirit. In fact, the Bible says that the very power that raised Jesus from the dead will be at work in your life (Ephesians 1:18-20). Jesus spoke of the wonderful presence of His Spirit in John 7:37-39:

"'If anyone is thirsty, let him come to me and drink. Whoever believes in me, as the Scripture has said, streams of living water will flow from within him.' By this he meant the Spirit . . ."

What did Jesus say we should do if we are thirsty for more of what He has for us?

_____

_____

How thirsty are you right now for a deeper work of God in your life?

☐ **Right now I am content and satisfied.**

☐ **I have a growing thirst for the power of God's spirit.**

☐ **I'm already very thirsty for a deeper work of God's spirit in me.**

☐ **Other:**

_____

Do you have any questions or fears about opening your life more fully to God's empowering presence? If so, what are they?

_____

_____

Take time when you meet with your mentor to discuss any questions you may have and to review your memory verses.

Unit 4, Day 1
Follow Jesus as Lord
Confess Jesus as Lord

JESUS IS LORD!

"That if you confess with your mouth, 'Jesus is Lord,' and believe in your heart that God raised him from the dead, you will be saved. For it is with your heart that you believe and are justified, and it is with your mouth that you confess and are saved" (Romans 10:9-10).

✎ **According to these verses, what two things does someone need to do to experience salvation?**

1. _____

2. _____

✎ **We don't use the word "Lord" much in modern English. What words do you think convey the same meaning in contemporary language?**

☐ **Director**   ☐ **Boss**   ☐ **Leader**

☐ **Friend**   ☐ **Priest**   ☐ **Other:** _____

According to Bible dictionaries, the word "Lord" means "owner, master . . . one who has full control of something." The word also carries the meaning of divine kingship.

To confess with your mouth that "Jesus is Lord" means to *personally declare* to others that Jesus is King and Master. He is who He claims to be — God's Son. More specifically, He is *your* leader and guide, the One you choose to take complete control of your life.

CONFESSING JESUS' LORDSHIP

Here are two other Bible passages that speak of confessing Christ. In these verses the word "acknowledge" means the same thing as the word "confess:"

"Whoever acknowledges me before men, I will also acknowledge him before my Father in heaven. But whoever disowns me before men, I will disown him before my Father in heaven" (Matthew 10:32-33).

"For if anyone acknowledges that Jesus is the Son of God, God lives in him and he in God" (1 John 4:15).

✎ **According to these verses, what are the promises for those who acknowledge or confess Jesus' Lordship?**

1. _____

2. _____

Imagine that you have recently developed a new friendship. You enjoy the company of this friend and he or she has confided that you are a special friend. Soon afterward, you overhear this person talking to someone else, not realizing that you are listening. Your new friend is critical of you and claims that you are *not* a friend. How would this make you feel?

✎ **What would you conclude about this person and your relationship? (Check all that would apply.)**

☐   **That he/she temporarily forgot my identity.**

☐   **That I am not really a best friend.**

☐   **That he/she is ashamed of me.**

☐   **That I cannot rely on this friendship.**

☐   **Other:** _____

Imagine the difference if you heard this person *praising* your qualities and proudly claiming your friendship. These words to others would reveal the true nature of the relationship with you. Jesus is saying this same thing about His Lordship and how you confess Him before others.

✎ **Name those you have already told about your new relationship with Christ:**

_____

_____

✎ **What were their various responses?**

_____

_____

✎ **How do you feel about confessing Christ to others who are close to you? (Check all that apply.)**

☐   **I am excited to share what Christ has done in my life.**

☐   **I am afraid to share with certain people.**

☐   **I am uncertain about how to share my relationship with Christ.**

☐   **I would like the prayer of my cell group as I confess Christ to family members and friends.**

☐   **All of the above.**

☐   **Other:** _____

_____

This week, memorize John 16:24. Review all other verses.

Unit 4, Day 2
Follow Jesus as Lord
Your Savior and Lord

SAVIOR AND LORD

Imagine you are swimming. You are far from the bank when you get a severe cramp in your side, crippling your ability to swim. About to drown, you scream, "Help! Help!" A strong swimmer hears your cry and rescues you.

Which word best describes your rescuer? (Mark your answer.)

☐   **My "Savior"**   ☐   **My "Lord"**

The fact that the swimmer saved you doesn't automatically make him your lord, does it? In order for him to be your lord, you would need to say:

"If it weren't for you, I wouldn't be alive. Therefore, I now give you my life. You have won the right to be my lord. Tell me where you want me to work and to live. I am your slave. You own my life. I will always love you for saving my life."

The center or heart of your will is like a throne. Before you became a Christian, you were the lord of your own life, ruling as a king from that throne. With no competition from any other person, you made every choice yourself. You rarely, if ever, consulted God. Like the rest of us, living life your own way led to many mistakes. You probably look back with regret at the pain you caused yourself and others by choosing to do things out of self-serving motives.

What were some of the results of living life with yourself as lord?

_____

_____

When you became a Christian, you gave your life to Jesus Christ to become not only your Savior, but also your Lord. That means you have given up all rights to your life. You continually confess, "Jesus is Lord!"

There are untold benefits to following Jesus as Lord. For the first time, you can live by God's plan. He never makes mistakes. You'll always have the best life can offer when you leave the choices up to Him! With Christ as Lord, you can experience the abundant life that He died to offer you. His presence working in your life will produce the *"fruit of the Spirit"* which is *"love, joy, peace, patience, kindness, gentleness, goodness, faithfulness and self-control"* (Galatians 5:22).

His guidance in your life will give you purpose and meaning.

ARE YOU STILL TRYING TO BE THE KING?

The writer of Psalms 119:72-73 understood the joy of being a servant to the Lord of Lords:

> *"The law from your mouth is more precious to me than thousands of pieces of silver and gold. Your hands made me and formed me; give me understanding to learn your commands."*

In Isaiah 29:16 the prophet describes someone who doesn't understand this truth:

> *"You turn things upside down, as if the potter were thought to be like the clay! Shall what is formed say to him who formed it, 'He did not make me?' Can the pot say of the potter, 'He knows nothing?'"*

The person addressed in this verse had a "throne room" that looked like this:

This type of Christian has accepted Jesus as Savior but is still wavering on whether He should be given exclusive rights to reign as Lord. The Bible calls such a Christian "worldly" or "double minded." People like this think that they are serving God, but the truth is, *"When Jesus is not Lord of all, He is not Lord at all!"*

It is a tragic thing to observe a Christian who receives the forgiveness for sin, yet continues to operate as a self-owned, self-governed person. The results are often tragic.

HAVE YOU SETTLED THE MATTER OF JESUS' LORDSHIP?

The worldly Christian never knows the deep things of God. This person's life is just a series of ups and downs without over-flowing joy or purpose. Strongholds are never broken. Sins are never confessed. Don't allow yourself to become like this!

Here's a prayer for you to constantly use:

> ***"Lord Jesus, I choose YOUR will in place of MY will. I gladly give YOU the throne of my heart and the rights to my life. I am YOUR servant."***

Are you prepared to let Him guide you in all the decisions you make? Can you pray those words right now? As you learn to listen to His voice, you will find great peace in knowing you are fulfilling His desires for your life. Because He loves you so deeply, following Him will bring you overflowing joy!

Today, be sure to review all the Scripture verses you have learned. Reflecting on them in your spare moments will make a great difference in your day.

Unit 4, Day 3
Follow Jesus as Lord
Declaring Jesus as Lord Through Baptism

THE CALL TO BE BAPTIZED

"Then Jesus came to them and said, 'All authority in heaven and on earth has been given to me. Therefore go and make disciples of all nations, baptizing them in the name of the Father and of the Son and of the Holy Spirit, and teaching them to obey everything I have commanded you. And surely I am with you always, to the very end of the age'" (Matthew 28:18–20).

These are Jesus' final words to His disciples in the Gospel of Matthew. Jesus left them with His presence and with His mission to "make disciples."

WHY IS BAPTISM IMPORTANT?

According to Jesus, water baptism is an essential part of following Him. It is a powerful way for us to declare His Lordship over our lives.

It is somewhat like a marriage commitment. When I proposed to my wife Ruth and gave her a diamond ring, I was expressing my love and commitment to her. The wedding ceremony, however, was also very important. By *publicly* declaring my commitment to her, I was saying that I belonged to her and that there was no turning back.

Baptism is like that. By being baptized, we declare to God, to ourselves and to others that Jesus is now Lord of our lives. Baptism is also God's way to express tangibly to you, "You are Mine. You are cleansed and forgiven. I love you! You belong to My family." That is why we are baptized "in the name of the Father and of the Son and of the Holy Spirit." These are more than words. They declare your new identity and belonging in Christ.

WHY WAIT?

"Those who accepted his message were baptized, and about three thousand were added to their number that day" (Acts 2:41).

"Then Philip began with that very passage of Scripture and told him the good news about Jesus. As they traveled along the road, they came to some water and the eunuch said, 'Look, here is water. Why shouldn't I be baptized?' Philip said, 'If you believe with all your heart, you may.' The eunuch answered, 'I believe that Jesus Christ is the Son of God.' And he gave orders to stop the chariot. Then both Philip and the eunuch went down into the water and Philip baptized him." (Acts 8:35 38)

What did the people in these passages do to qualify for baptism?

_____

_____

Perhaps in the past you were baptized as an infant or simply as a ritual to join a church. Centuries of religious tradition have often corrupted the teaching of the Bible. Baptism is a way for you to declare that you believe in Jesus Christ and received Him as Lord. Infants cannot do that. Since you have taken Christ as Lord, you now qualify for baptism for the first time in your life.

In the passages on page 40, when does it say that the new believers were baptized?

☐ **After several months had passed**

☐ **As soon as possible**

☐ **On Easter Sunday**

In Scripture, there is *never* an example of people delaying baptism. Once you believe in Christ and turn to Him, there is no reason to wait to confess Jesus as your Lord through the witness of baptism.

Some new Christians may say, "I don't want to offend a relative by being baptized." They should ask instead, "How offended will my Lord be if I put my relatives above *Him*? Am I ashamed of my commitment to Christ? Will my relatives ever choose to follow Jesus if I do not let them know I have made a life-changing decision?"

(Note: Children and teens in a non-Christian home, however, should discuss baptism with their parents and get their permission before being baptized. Scripture says we are to honor our parents. This is the only Scriptural reason to delay baptism.)

What questions do you have about baptism? Jot them down to discuss with your mentor:

_____

_____

_____

DECISION: it is my desire to be baptized on (date) _____

Guests I will invite to witness my baptism:

_____

_____

_____

_____

_____

_____

_____

_____

Unit 4, Day 4
Follow Jesus as Lord
Who's the Master? Who's the Servant?

WHO'S IN CHARGE HERE?

Often when Christians come to God in prayer they have myriad requests. "God, heal my mother." "Help me excel at school or work." "Bless my marriage." "Give me wisdom and patience." In the midst of our requests, we may be tempted to think of God as our servant — someone we have added to our life for our own blessing and convenience.

God loves us deeply and delights to hear our requests. But we must always realize that *we are the servants* and *He is the Master.* As our loving Master, He will provide and take care of us. As His servants, our first concern is to hear His voice and respond in joyful obedience.

The words of the boy Samuel in the Old Testament capture the heart of this submission to God:

"Speak, Lord, for your servant is listening" (1 Samuel 3:10).

In the New Testament, Mary expressed this same heart. When an angel announced that she would give birth to Jesus, God's Son, she responded:

"I am the Lord's servant. May it be to me as you have said" (Luke 1:38).

 Who did Samuel and Mary view as their master?

_____

 What word did they use to describe themselves?

_____

REVERSING THE TRIANGLE

The first triangle on the facing page illustrates the way non-Christians relate to the spiritual world. Maybe it describes your own past experience. To understand the diagram, follow these instructions. First, study the triangle:

 Write your name in the blank above the word "master."

Before individuals receive Christ, they play a role in which they are masters of their life, deciding "what's best."

 Now write the word "gods" in the blank below the word "servant."

Lacking the ability to bring their desires to pass, unbelievers choose some sort of god to bring them power or guidance to fulfill their own wishes. Their god, however, is not their *master*. They do not ask, "What is your will for my life?" Their *god* is a servant to help them accomplish their own goals, what they as lord of their own lives choose as "what's best."

Now write in the words "medium or priest" below the word "manipulator."

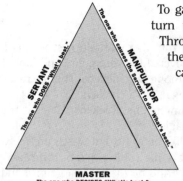

To gain more access to the spiritual, the unbeliever can turn to a go-between, like a spiritist, guru or priest. Through rituals or sacrifices, these "holy men" will help the person manipulate the spiritual beings. This is, basically, the way all non-Christian religions work. This includes Hinduism and cults, the occult and the New Age movement. People are trying to gain power and direction by controlling and appeasing spiritual forces. However, they remain the masters of their own lives. Their gods are little more than puppets to help them on their way.

THE CHRISTIAN TRIANGLE TURNS EVERYTHING UPSIDE DOWN
When we receive Christ, we crown Him as Master of our lives.

 Write "Jesus" in the blank under "master" in the diagram shown below.

When Jesus is *Master*, you and I now become servants. Jesus *decides* "what's best," and we stand ready to do "what's best!" Unlike the first triangle, this one has a special ingredient, the Listening Room. The most important part of being a servant is listening for our Master's instructions. That's why taking time in the Listening Room, reading the Bible and hearing God's voice through the fellow members of our cell group is so important.

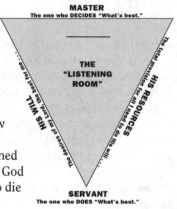

Unlike the first triangle, where rituals are performed to gain the favor of spiritual forces, now we have a God who already loves us so much that He sent His Son to die for us. As Paul wrote,

"He who did not spare his own Son, but gave Him up for us all — how will he not also along with him, graciously give us all things?" (Romans 8:32)

 Now, write your own name under "servant!"

 What situation are you facing today where you need to hear the master's voice? Write a prayer below expressing submission to his will:

_____

_____

_____

Unit 4, Day 5
Follow Jesus as Lord
Your Riches in Christ

BE WHO YOU ARE IN CHRIST!

According to an African story, an eagle chick fell from its mountain nest during a night storm when it was only days old. A farmer discovered the young bird and took it home. When he had nursed it to health, he placed it among his chickens. Though made to soar in the sky, this gorgeous bird grew up thinking it was a chicken.

One day a friend saw the now full-grown bird among the chickens. He told the farmer, "That large bird among your chickens is an eagle!"

But the man only laughed. He said, "No. It looks like an eagle, but watch it closely. It walks like a chicken, scratches like a chicken and eats like a chicken. *It is a chicken!*"

The friend said, "Let me prove that it is an eagle." And he took the large bird and tossed it in the air. But the bird only meekly flapped its large wings and then landed among the chickens and preceded to scratch the ground in search of bugs. The farmer and his children laughed. But the friend was undeterred. He again captured the bird and using a ladder, climbed up on the thatched roof of the farmer's hut. He said to the bird, "Fly, Eagle! Fly! You are not of the earth but of the sky!" And he tossed the bird as high as he could. But the eagle merely glanced at the chickens below, stretched its powerful wings and glided to the ground to resume its scratching.

The farmer shouted, "See, I told you it was a chicken." And he and his family roared with laughter. The friend returned home.

The farmer was jarred from his sleep the next morning by a knock on his door. When he opened the door and peered out in the darkness, he saw his friend and moaned, "What are you doing here so early in the morning?"

The friend replied, "I want to show you something. Bring your funny bird and follow me." The farmer reluctantly fetched the bird and followed. In the cool morning darkness, they climbed the steep trail to the top of the mountain where the farmer had originally found the eaglet. Just as the sun was about to rise, they reached a ledge of rock near the summit.

The friend then took the bird and gently set it down on the edge of the ledge so that the bird faced east. He spoke softly and firmly, "Look at the sun, O Eagle, and as it rises, rise with it. You belong to the sky not to the earth. Fly, Eagle, fly!" Just then the sun broke the horizon across the river valley below, dazzling them in its warm glow. The eagle gazed at the rising sun, raised its head, stretched its wings and slowly leaned over the ledge. Then feeling the updraft of a wind more powerful than man or bird, it swept up, soaring higher and higher in the brightness of the morning sun, never again to live among the chickens.

This story illustrates a powerful truth about *you*. You now belong to Christ. Jesus lives in you and you are a new creation in Him!

Satan's only hope is to keep you confused about who you really are. In fact, the name "Satan" means *the accuser*. He wants you to believe lies to make you think that you are un-important or unloved or unforgiven. As you read the Bible, you will discover that God wants you to know who you truly are in Him so that you may experience all He has for you.

Ponder these truths about yourself from God's word, reading them aloud to yourself:

- I have been put right with God by faith and have peace with Him. (Romans 5:1)
- I have been saved by Christ's life. (Romans 5:10)
- I have died to sin. (Romans 6:2)
- I now have no condemnation. (Romans 8:1)
- I am called into fellowship with Jesus Christ my Lord. (1 Corinthians 1:9)
- I will put on immortality. (1 Corinthians 15:53)
- I am comforted by God. (2 Corinthians 1:4)
- I have been given God's Spirit as a pledge. (2 Corinthians 1:22)
- I have received mercy. (2 Corinthians 4:1)
- I have a house not made with hands in the heavens. (2 Corinthians 5:1)
- I am a new creation in Christ. The old has gone, the new is come. (2 Corinthians 5:17)
- I am Christ's ambassador. (2 Corinthians 5:20)
- I am holy and blameless in God's sight. (Ephesians 1:4)
- I am God's child. (Ephesians 1:5)
- I am a citizen in God's kingdom and a member of His family. (Ephesians 2:19)
- I can approach God with confidence to find grace and mercy in time of need. (Hebrews 4:16)
- God will never leave me nor forsake me. (Hebrews 13:5)
- According to God's great mercy, I have been born again into a living hope through the resurrection of Jesus Christ from the dead. (1 Peter 1:3)
- I have been given an inheritance which is imperishable, undefiled and unfading — kept in heaven for me. (1 Peter 1:4)
- I was not redeemed with perishable things like silver and gold, but by the blood of Christ, like a lamb without blemish or defect. (1 Peter 1:18–19)

Read these truths aloud two more times. As you do, <u>underline</u> those that stand out to you as especially important for you right now.

Based on these truths, write down, in your own words, who you are:

I am: _____

_____

_____

_____

_____

_____

If anyone is in Christ, he is a new creation; the old has gone, the new has come! 2 Corinthians 5:17

Unit 5, Day 1
Grow in God's Word
The Power of God's Word

GOD'S WORD CHANGES LIVES AND HISTORY

In 1517 in Germany, a monk and professor of theology named Martin Luther was studying the book of Romans. Through the medieval church, Luther learned that salvation was earned through good works, church rituals, and acts of penance. But as he read the book of Romans, a light flooded the darkness as he realized salvation was a free gift an individual received by faith. He later wrote,

> *"I grasped the truth that the righteousness of God is that righteousness whereby, through grace and sheer mercy, He justifies us by faith. Thereupon I felt myself to be reborn and to have gone through open doors into paradise."*

God's Word spoke with power to Luther, changing not only his life, but the course of history, as he declared the message of salvation to his generation. He set in motion the great Reformation movement that revolutionized the church of his day.

The transforming power of God's Word has been demonstrated countless times around the world and through the ages. It changes our lives and through us our worlds.

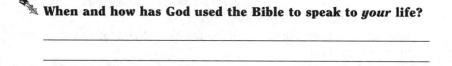 **When and how has God used the Bible to speak to *your* life?**

_____

_____

POWER TO TRANSFORM

Your mind is like a powerful computer. A computer, no matter how advanced and powerful, is no more useful than the programs it contains. You can have a perfect computer, but if you load a faulty or "buggy" program on it, it will function defectively. A common comment about computers is, "Garbage in, garbage out."

In a sense, that is how our minds operate. Formerly, we loaded our wonderful, God-given brains with defective thought patterns, attitudes, and values, which led us in the wrong direction. Now, God offers us the power to reprogram our minds with His Word, the Bible, which will lead us in the right direction. As Jesus says in John 8:32,

> *"If you hold to my teaching, you are really my disciples. Then you will know the truth and the truth will set you free."*

In a different way, Romans 12:2 declares the same reality:

> *"Do not conform any longer to the pattern of this world, but be transformed by the renewing of your mind. Then you will be able to test and approve what God's will is — His good, pleasing and perfect will."*

🖋 **According to this verse, how will your life be further transformed?**

_____

_____

_____

🖋 **What is the benefit of letting your life be transformed?**

_____

_____

_____

🖋 **According to this passage, what are the characteristics of God's will for your life? It is . . . (Check all that apply)**

- ☐ **Good (right and true)**
- ☐ **Pleasing (deeply satisfying)**
- ☐ **Boring (repetitive and meaningless)**
- ☐ **Perfect (wonderfully fitted to you)**

Did you check all the answers except the third one? God has wonderful plans for you! You'll be discovering them more and more deeply as you let your mind be renewed by His Word.

THE RICHES OF GOD'S WORD

"The law of the Lord is perfect, reviving the soul.
The statutes of the Lord are trustworthy, making wise the simple.
The precepts of the Lord are right, giving joy to the heart.
The commands of the Lord are radiant, giving light to the eyes.
The fear of the Lord is pure enduring forever.
The ordinances of the Lord are sure and altogether righteous.
They are more precious than gold, than much pure gold;
they are sweeter than honey, than honey from the cone.
By keeping them is your servant warned; in keeping them there is great reward."
Psalms 19:7-11

🖋 **What benefits of God's word, listed in the verses above, speak to you right now as you read and meditate on this passage?**

_____

_____

Begin to memorize this week's Scripture memory verses: 2 Corinthians 10:3-4 and Proverbs 3:5-6.

Unit 5, Day 2
Grow in God's Word
Versions of the Bible: Which One?

WHICH VERSION?

The Old Testament, the part of the Bible written before Christ came to Earth, was originally written in Hebrew, the language of the Israeli people. The New Testament, the part written after Christ came, was written in Greek, the dominant international language of that day.

Today, we have many excellent versions of the Bible available in English. You may ask, "Which version is best?" The answer is, "It depends." Different versions achieve different purposes. There are two basic kinds of English Bibles: translations and paraphrases. Translations carefully convert the original text into English word for word. Paraphrases convey the original message meaning for meaning.

Translations are great for memorizing or studying the Bible. Paraphrases are wonderful for personal and family devotional reading. It is hard to say which version is best for you now. You may want to have a main version that you use most of the time and then also get one or two others that you use for a change of pace or when you want to study a passage more deeply. To help you make a choice, below are excerpts and comments on some of the most popular versions. To make comparison easy, we will examine Psalms 1:1-2 from different translations:

TRANSLATIONS

New International Version

> *"Blessed is the man who does not walk in the counsel of the wicked or stand in the way of sinners or sit in the seat of mockers. But his delight is in the law of the LORD and on his law he meditates day and night."*

The New International is perhaps the most popular of modern translations. It is the version used throughout this book and for your Scripture memory verses. It is both accurate and clear.

King James Version

> *"Blessed is the man that walketh not in the counsel of the ungodly, nor standeth in the way of sinners, nor sitteth in the seat of the scornful. But his delight is in the law of the LORD; and in his law doth he meditate day and night."*

The King James was the standard English translation for centuries. Its poetic language is beautiful, but most modern readers find it difficult to read and understand.

Good News Bible

> *"Happy are those who reject the advice of evil men, who do not follow the example of sinners or join those who have no use for God. Instead, they find joy in obeying the Law of the LORD, and they study it day and night."*

This translation was written for those using English as a second language — as did the audience of the original New Testament books, many of whom used Greek as a second language. It is simple and straightforward.

PARAPHRASES

The Living Bible

"Oh, the joys of those who do not follow evil men's advice, who do not hang around with sinners, scoffing at the things of God: But they delight in doing everything God wants them to, and day and night are always meditating on his laws and thinking about ways to follow him more closely."

This popular paraphrase was written for children but has made God's Word real to millions, both young and old.

The Message

"How well God must like you — you don't hang out at Sin Saloon, you don't slink along Dead-End Road, you don't go to Smart-Mouth College. Instead you thrill to Yahweh's Word, you chew on Scripture day and night."

This paraphrase was done by poet and author Eugene Peterson. Its fresh, captivating language is great for personal and family devotions, but it is frustrating for serious study because similar words and phrases in the original passages are sometimes rendered in very different ways.

In reading Psalms 1:1-2 in the versions given above, what stands out to you from this passage of God's word?

_____

_____

Which version or versions appeal to you the most from the samples above?

_____

_____

What do you think you need most in a version of the Bible right now?

- ☐ An accurate translation.
- ☐ A version that speaks to me in simple English.
- ☐ A Bible with fresh, dynamic language for personal and family devotions.
- ☐ I already have a Bible that fits my needs now.
- ☐ I would like one or two more versions so that I can enjoy and study God's word more deeply.
- ☐ Other: _____

Unit 5, Day 3
Grow in God's Word
Your Daily Listening Room

HOW'S IT GOING?

In Week 2 of this study, you began learning how to hear
God's voice by establishing your own Listening Room. In Day 5 of that week you were
encouraged to set aside a special time and place in your daily schedule to spend with
God and to hear His words of encouragement and instruction to you.

How has it gone for you?

- [ ] **Not very well. My times with God have been few and far between.**
- [ ] **I have had rich times of study, prayer and listening to God, but it has been inconsistent, not daily.**
- [ ] **I have my Listening Room time with God almost daily and it has been enriching and empowering.**
- [ ] **Other:** _____

If consistent time with Christ has been a challenge to you, what has been the major obstacle or obstacles?

- [ ] **I am too busy.**
- [ ] **There are too many interruptions.**
- [ ] **It has not been important to me.**
- [ ] **I don't know how to structure the time.**
- [ ] **Other:** _____

How might you eliminate or minimize these obstacles?

Today, you will learn a flexible format to use during your Listening Room time.
Realize, however, that this format is here to *serve* you. It is your *servant*, not your master. There will be times that you deviate from it as God calls you to spend more time in
one area or another. The format, however, is freeing because instead of thinking about
what to do next, you can focus on Christ and what He is speaking to your heart.

BEGIN WITH WORSHIP (At least 5 minutes)

Bow at the feet of your Master, giving Him your thanks and worship. You may want
to sing praise songs or listen to worship music. Don't stop until you feel His presence!

OPEN YOUR SPIRIT IN PRAYER (At least 1-minute)

Invite God to speak to you and teach you as you look into His Word. Jesus promised
that He would send the Holy Spirit to guide you into all truth (John 16:13). Pray

something like this: *"Holy Spirit, I thank You that You are my Teacher. You are welcome in every area of my life. Open my spiritual eyes to discover everything You want to show me."*

READ AND LISTEN (At least 15 minutes)

Carefully read the verses that you have selected for the day. What is the point of the passage? How does it apply to your life? Does a word or phrase stand out to you? You may want to underline a verse or phrase in your Bible, writing in the margin the date or situation that made it important to you. As you read, ponder: "What is the Holy Spirit teaching me through this Scripture?"

Over the next months you may consider memorizing the verses you selected for the day. Rather than tackling huge sections of the Bible, focus on a few verses. This "less is more" approach may help you find freedom instead of frustration in your on-going Christian growth.

You may also consider writing a journal during the times when you read the Bible.

KEEP A JOURNAL (Include in your READ AND LISTEN time)

Buy a blank book or notebook. Let it be your spiritual diary. Note thoughts and impressions given to you by the Holy Spirit. Make it very personal! It is for your eyes only. Like the psalmist, write down your joys and frustrations in prayer to God.

PRAY (Whatever time you desire and have available)

Many Christians have found rich blessing in spending an hour a day in prayer. If you cannot do this daily, try doing it one day a week at first. Saturday or Sunday morning may be a good choice for you. The one-hour pattern given below is intended to be flexible. It is there to serve you, not to control you. Each of the blocks of time can be 10 minutes. Or, you may want to expand or abbreviate the amount of time given to each section. The pattern moves outward and then inward: *outward,* as you praise God and pray for those over you in the church and government and *inward* as you pray for friends, family and yourself.

- *Worship God*
- *Pray for your Pastor, Church and cell members*
- *Pray for your government*
- *Pray for friends that need to follow Christ*
- *Pray for family members*
- *Pray for yourself*

What do you see as the next step for you as you grow closer to God in prayer?

_____

_____

Continue to work on this week's memory verses: 2 Corinthians 10:3-4 and Proverbs 3:5-6.

Unit 5, Day 4
Grow in God's Word
Go Deeper in God's Word

THE RICHES OF GOD'S WORD

> *"But as for you, continue in what you have learned and have become convinced of, because you know from whom you learned it, and how from infancy you have known the holy Scriptures, which are able to make you wise for salvation through faith in Christ Jesus. All Scripture is God-breathed and is useful for teaching, rebuking, correcting and training in righteousness, so that the man of God may be equipped for every good work" (2 Timothy 3:14-17).*

This passage encourages you to continue and go deeper in God's Word. You are now a babe in Christ, born into God's family. Let His Word nurture you and help you grow into the fullness of all He has for you.

According to these verses, what will the study of Scripture do for your life?

_____

_____

In addition to your regular reading and reflecting on the Bible, there will be times that you will want to dig more deeply into God's Word. Maybe you will be facing a decision or a struggle in your life and you'll want to learn God's perspective on a certain issue. Or, perhaps you will simply get caught up in the joy of studying a certain book or topic in Scripture. There are many special Bibles and study tools which will help you dig deeper in the treasure of God's Word. Here are some you may want to obtain in the months ahead:

STUDY BIBLES
Study Bibles are loaded with notes, maps, charts and helpful comments. There are a wide variety available. The *NIV Study Bible is* particularly helpful. It has notes at the bottom of each page related to each particular passage. When you use it you will feel like you are accompanied by Bible scholars helping you understand difficult thoughts.

A simpler study Bible is called *The Student Bible*. Designed for newcomers to the Bible, it has excellent introductions to each book of the Bible. Instead of extensive notes, it has catchy "highlights" inserted between passages that help explain facts and draw your attention into the text. It also has a subject guide in the back to help you look up and explore verses related to topics of interest.

TOPICAL BIBLES

A topical Bible provides verses by subjects, gathered from all the books of the Bible. The most popular Bible of this type is *The New Nave's Topical Bible*. Another study Bible that doubles as a topical Bible is *The Thompson Chain Reference Bible*. It lets you follow "chains" of Scriptures on thousands of topics throughout the Bible. These chains can also be found under topical headings in the back of the Bible.

COMPUTER RESOURCES

The electronic age offers amazing possibilities for Bible study! If you want to search for all the listings of a certain word or phrase in the Bible, a computer Bible program can find in seconds what used to take hours or even days to find with printed texts. The verses can then be cut and pasted to other documents for further study. In addition to the Bible text, these programs offer maps and Bible commentaries. If you use a personal computer, you may want to get a Bible program. One excellent shareware program available on Internet for both the PC and Mac platforms is *The Online Bible*.

Retail computer programs include *Quick Verse, PC Study Bible, WORD Search, Lesson Maker,* and *MY BIBLE* for your Palm Handheld.

BIBLE DICTIONARIES AND ENCYCLOPEDIAS

These books allow you to look up Bible characters, locations, and themes to get rich background details. You may want to buy a dictionary or encyclopedia in the future. *The New Bible Dictionary* and the five-volume *Zondervan Pictorial Encyclopedia of the Bible* are excellent resources.

GOD'S WORD TO YOU THOUGH YOUR PASTOR

> *"They (the new Christians) devoted themselves to the apostles' teaching and to the fellowship, to the breaking of bread and to prayer" (Acts 2:42).*

 Underline the first thing mentioned in this verse that the new Christians were devoted to.

Notice from this verse that new believers in the early church learned from their leaders. God's word is "useful for teaching, rebuking, correcting and training in right-eousness" (2 Timothy 3:16). God has appointed leaders in the church to teach His Word to you. Sometimes God will speak through them to encourage you. At other times, their message will bring challenge, correction or rebuke. As you listen with an open heart to sermons and teachings, always take notes. Studies show that taking notes more than doubles what you learn and remember. Your cell group will discuss the sermon topics each week. Taking notes will help you remember truths your cell group will discuss during your weekly meeting.

This week, take simple notes from your pastor's Sunday message. What stands out to you? How is God speaking to you? Share your thoughts and notes with your mentor.

Unit 5, Day 5
Grow in God's Word
Where Do You Go From Here?

CONGRATULATIONS!

Today marks the last day in this study. By completing it, you have shown that you are serious about growing and going on to receive everything Christ has for you! Be sure to ask your mentor to sign the "Verification of Completion." Show this signed document to your cell group leader. Let's review what follows this booklet:

LIFE IN CHRIST'S BODY

"From him (Christ) the whole body, joined and held together by every supporting ligament, grows and builds itself up in love as each part does its work" (Ephesians 4:16).

Which of the statements below are taught in Ephesians 4:16?

☐ **We grow in Christ when we are joined to others.**

☐ **Mutual love is vital to building each other up.**

☐ **As in a human body, each part of Christ's body is important to its health and growth.**

☐ **All of the above.**

Notice in this verse that the body of Christ grows as each part does its work. That includes you! You are a special part of your cell group. Your unique gifts and abilities are important for your group to become all that God wants it to be. You need to both give and receive. Here are some important points for you for living in your new family.

1. PRAY FOR THE CELL MEMBERS.

God's Word says, *"Confess your sins to each other and pray for each other so that you may be healed. The prayer of a righteous person is powerful and effective" (James 5:16).* You will see many miracles as you pray for the concerns of your fellow cell members.

2. BUILD FRIENDSHIPS.

One of the best parts of cell life is friendship. Build friendship with your cell members by involving them in recreational activities in your life and by sharing times of fun and work together. Don't just wait for others to reach out to you. Take the initiative in building deeper relationships with them.

3. FORGIVE.

As in all families, those in your cell group will sometimes irritate and offend you. Remember God's encouragement:

"Be kind and compassionate to one another, forgiving each other, just as in Christ God forgave you" (Ephesians 4:32).

To your ministry ↓

VERIFICATION OF COMPLETION

As the Facilitator for

(Name of cell group member:) _____

I have reviewed the attendance records for *Beginning the Journey* and I certify

that the course has been completed.

Signed: _____

Date: _____

HOW TO SERVE AS A MENTOR

Welcome to one of the most important tasks you will ever do in your life — providing spiritual care and guidance to a new believer. What a privilege and responsibility! Your care for this person will help him or her lay the foundation for a lifetime of serving Christ. This "Mentor's Guide" will assist you in your assignment. It will also help *you* grow. Nothing is more exciting than walking with a new Christian through the joys, discoveries, and struggles of his or her journey.

Your assignment is to encourage and support this new cell group member. You are there to be a friend and to pray for him or her. It's not necessary for you to demonstrate perfection. (If that were required, no one could be a mentor!)

You are neither a teacher nor an expert as a mentor. Just be a caring brother or sister in Christ. It will be far more important for you to *listen* than to *instruct*.

Sometimes your Protégé may have questions you can't answer. That is to be expected. Be transparent and explain you will try to find an answer for both of you.

Sometimes you may feel like *you* are the one who needs prayer. If so, give your Protégé opportunity to pray for you. Learning to pray for others is vital to our spiritual development.

GETTING TO KNOW YOUR PROTÉGÉ

Hopefully, you already know this new believer. Perhaps you were present when your cell group leader visited this new believer. If this interview has not taken place, it should happen as soon as possible. Tell your cell group leader that you are anxious to go along for this important visit to the Protégé.

In addition to your weekly sharing time with your Protégé, you are encouraged to enjoy other times together. What activities could you do together or with other cell members? Perhaps you might have some meals together, go to a concert or a sporting event. You might also want to shop, exercise or sit together at your celebration service.

The closer your relationship becomes, the more powerfully Christ will use you to support and encourage one another. Be one of the first persons in your cell group to bond to this new believer.

WHEN AND WHERE TO MEET

You can meet almost any time and anywhere. Talk about this with your Protégé. The important thing is to set aside at least one hour with each other each week for the next five weeks. This can be done in the morning before work, over lunch, in the evening or on weekends. Another option is to meet just before or after your cell meeting or celebration service. As a mentor, you should set aside at least one hour of personal time to pray and prepare for each session together. It is very important that you do not put this preparation off to the last minute because there will often be key tasks for you to do mid-week.

UNIT 1 — WELCOME TO YOUR NEW JOURNEY!

PREPARE FOR YOUR TIME TOGETHER

1. Make sure your Protégé has a copy of this booklet. Ask the Protégé to read and complete Unit One (pages 4-13). Emphasize the importance of using a pen or pencil to respond to the questions in each Unit.

2. Pray for your Protégé and your times together. Ask God to give both of you a deeper hunger for Him. Invite the Holy Spirit to open your eyes to a fuller knowledge of your Protégé's needs. Thank Him for what He is going to do.

YOUR TIMES TOGETHER

Your times with the new believer should not take the form of a lecture, seminar or interview. Be sensitive to the Protégé's needs. Do not get sidetracked on unimportant matters. Your sharing times should be for sharing about life as a Christian. Feel free to share insights, victories and needs from your own life, but remember to do a lot more listening than talking. In the outline below, time frames are given to help you pace your sharing with each other.

1. GET BETTER-ACQUAINTED (12 MINUTES).

To learn more about each other, share answers with one another using the questions below:

- Where did you live between the ages of 7 and 10 and how many brothers and sisters did you have?
- What was the spiritual climate of your family during those years?
- What people or circumstances influenced your desire to become a Christian?
- What is your current life situation in terms of family, work and interests?

2. PRAY AND MINISTER (5 MINUTES).

Explain it is important to welcome the Lord and to invite Him to guide your sharing times together. Lead in a simple prayer. If the new believer is not used to praying, guide him or her to also pray a simple prayer, thanking Jesus for His presence with you.

Help your Protégé get into the habit of conversing easily with Jesus at any time. A prayer life is not taught — it's caught! Unbelievers are "God-shy;" each new believer must be taught how to come boldly before His presence. Share examples of how God has answered prayer for you.

If you have listened carefully to your Protégé in the getting acquainted time, you may already be aware of inner needs. Don't be afraid to stop at any point in your sharing times to talk to the Holy Spirit about issues that have surfaced. Your Protégé will probably learn as much from the *way* you pray as from what you are praying *about*.

3. REVIEW UNIT 1 (20 MINUTES).

Look at Unit 1, Day 2 with your Protégé. Did he or she answer the questions on pages 6-7 using a pen or pencil? If not, ask him or her to complete the questions at this time.

Explain how important it is to answer by using a pen or pencil. Explain that the questions are there to stimulate learning. Research reveals that we remember almost six times as much if we actually *write down* our answers instead of just responding mentally. It is worth the extra effort!

Talk about the response to the first question. How did your Protégé view God in the past? How does that picture match the truth about God revealed in Scripture? Don't expect a baby Christian to have a mature concept of God. Misconceptions may have come from wrong teaching or no previous religious experience.

Look at the response to the question on "sin." Does your Protégé understand that sin is deeper than our actions and words? It is rebellion against God's authority and love. This will be discussed from every possible angle in the daily growth guides.

Review Unit 1, Day 5, discussing the importance of the cell group in the life of a believer. Share your own story of what life in the cell has meant to you.

4. WITNESS THE SIGNING OF "MY PERSONAL COVENANT" (5 MINUTES).

Invite the new believer to sign "My Personal Covenant" on page 13 if this has not already been done. This gives your Protégé an opportunity to submit more fully to the control of Jesus. It also expresses a commitment to the cell group and a desire to journey into spiritual maturity. Seal the signing of the commitment with a prayer of blessing.

5. DISCUSS SPENDING TIME DAILY WITH CHRIST (7 MINUTES).

Encourage your Protégé to spend time daily with Jesus. This is very important. Emphasize that Christ is within us, so we can speak to Him at anytime. He is interested in every aspect of our lives and wants an intimate relationship with each of us.

What time of the day would be best for the Protégé to set aside for the Listening Room experience? Establish a *specific time* each day for this to take place. Over the next weeks, the new believer will use the daily guides in this booklet. In Unit 5 of this booklet, we will learn more about Bible study and the advantages of using different Bible translations.

Share about your own daily encounter with Christ. Give examples of what it has meant to you.

6. REVIEW THE SCRIPTURE MEMORY VERSE (5 MINUTES).

Has your Protégé memorized this week's verses, 1 John 5:11-12? Repeat them together now. Discuss their meaning.

7. PLAN YOUR NEXT GET-TOGETHER (6 MINUTES).

Did the time and location of this week's get-together work well? When should you meet together next week?

Share significant events and related prayer concerns coming up in your lives in the next week. Conclude by coming to Christ together in prayer.

Emphasize the importance of completing Unit 2 before you meet together next week.

(As a mentor, you should begin today to get ready for the next session by reviewing the Mentor's Guide for Unit 2.)

UNIT 2 — HOW TO LISTEN TO YOUR LORD

PREPARE FOR YOUR TIME TOGETHER

1. Some time this week, phone your Protégé to see how things are going. What is happening in his or her life? Is there anything new that you should be praying for? If so, take time to pray together over the phone. Is the Protégé progressing through Unit 2? Confirm your meeting time and place.

2. Go over Unit 2 yourself and review the memory verses. Think about personal experiences that you would like to share — events in your own Listening Room times that will confirm you, too, have found this daily time with the Lord to be valuable.

3. Continue to pray for your Protégé, inviting the Spirit to more deeply reveal His abundant love. Ask God to direct you as you prepare for your meeting.

YOUR TIME TOGETHER

1. SHARE PERSONALLY WITH EACH OTHER (10 MINUTES).

Begin by talking about the least sensitive issues. How did your Protégé's week go? Was there an event at home or work or school that overshadowed the rest of their week? Although you are there to minister, don't hide your own emotions and needs. This nurtures the bond between you and nothing will help your Protégé grow more than ministering to you!

Ask about his or her prayer life over the past week. If things have not gone well, don't scold but encourage. If he or she sets aside special time for prayer only twice in the past week, that may be gigantic progress in contrast to the week before.

Listen with sensitivity to what is shared, and with your "spiritual ears" listen for what the Lord will say to you about special areas needing ministry.

2. REVIEW YOUR MEMORY VERSES (5 MINUTES).

Say your memory verses together, 1 John 5:11-12, without reference to the verse card. Your Protégé should have also begun memorizing the second verse, 1 Corinthians 10:13. Practice it together.

3. DISCUSS UNIT 2 ABOUT "THE LISTENING ROOM" (30 MINUTES).

Sit beside your Protégé during this part of your meeting so that you can look at the booklet and the answers together.

What stood out to your Protégé in this Unit? What truths seemed new and important?

What questions are there about what was studied? Is there anything that was hard to understand?

Did your Protégé sense God speaking through the exercises on pages 15, 17 and 19? Look at the responses that were written in the booklet. If he or she didn't sense anything in particular, that is all right. The first step is sometimes just learning how to be quiet before God.

"Where Is God When You Commune With Him?" Did this lesson from Day 2, pages 16-17, speak to your Protégé? The Creator of the Universe has come to live in his or her life! Emphasize that God is always speaking. Review how the Protégé "heard" the voice of the Lord at the time of his or her decision to accept Christ.

Discuss the role of God's Word as a "tuning fork," mentioned on page 19. We do not want to accept every impression that we get as coming from God. Scripture alone acts as the ultimate guide for us to assess the feelings and ideas that come to us.

Look together at the questions in Day 5 on pages 22-23. Take time to discuss each response in order to help your Protégé establish a meaningful personal Listening Room.

4. PRAY AND MINISTER TO EACH OTHER (10 MINUTES).

Now that you have discussed listening to God's voice, let Him give you insights on how to pray for each other. Open your prayer time by asking for God's Spirit to direct you in prayer and ministry. Then follow His guidance as you pray for one another. This may be the beginning of true intercessory prayer in the life of your Protégé.

5. PLAN YOUR NEXT GET-TOGETHER (5 MINUTES).

Clarify when and where you will meet next week. Will the same arrangement work again? Commit yourselves to pray for each other in the meantime. Emphasize the importance of completing Unit 3 before you meet again.

Begin today to get ready for your time together next week by reading the "Prepare for Your Time Together" section for Unit 3.

UNIT 3 — RECEIVE CHRIST'S FREEDOM

PREPARE FOR YOUR TIME TOGETHER

1. As you review Unit 3 in preparation for your time with your Protégé, invite the Holy Spirit to search your heart and mind. Are there strongholds — attitudes, resentments, beliefs — that are holding *you* back from everything God has for you? If so, bring them to God. If you need the help of someone else, call your cell leader or a trusted, mature believer to pray together with you.

2. Continue to pray for your Protégé, asking the Holy Spirit to continue His work of revealing Christ's love, power and freedom in this new Christian's life. Pray for guidance as you prepare for your sharing time.

3. The need for your Protégé to be tied into your cell group cannot be overemphasized. Think of activities you can use to accomplish this.

YOUR TIME TOGETHER

1. SHARE PERSONALLY WITH EACH OTHER (10 MINUTES).

Begin by sharing with each other how your week has been. Don't spend too long on this unless there is a matter for ministry. Move into the subject of this study by asking, "What was the most difficult thing you've ever had to do?" (Be ready to share your own most difficult moment.) Then ask, "What has been the hardest change for you since becoming a Christian?" (If the first answer already covers this, omit this second question.) The Protégé's answer will probably indicate where he or she is having a struggle. It will take a few sessions for you to fully sense the way this person feels about life's problems.

Don't attempt to minister to this struggle right now. That will come later. Instead, if it is appropriate, move directly into a review of the verses being memorized.

2. REVIEW YOUR MEMORY VERSES (5 MINUTES).

Review the memory verses from the first two units, 1 John 5:11-12 and 1 Corinthians 10:13, saying them aloud with your Protégé. Then go over the memory verse for this week, 1 John 1:9.

3. DISCUSS UNIT 3 ABOUT RECEIVING JESUS' FREEDOM (30 MINUTES).

Ask: "Do you remember what we learned about sin and sins two weeks ago?" Let the Protégé tell you in his or her own words. Be patient. Discern if he or she has the right idea. The right words are less important than grasping the concept.

Look at the diagram on page 24 and explore its meaning. You may need to jog his or her memory with a question like, "Which is the root and which is the fruit?" Make sure it is understood that sin is an attitude of the heart that leads to a lifestyle in which God has no authority. The Christian is no longer to have that attitude, but can still be affected by it — and that means we still commit sins.

To what extent does God forgive and cleanse us when we confess our sins? Emphasize the truth of God's total forgiveness. Even sins as horrendous as King David's adultery and murder can be instantly forgiven when we admit our guilt.

What is a stronghold? Does your Protégé understand this concept? If not, review the material on pages 26-27. A "little child" does not become a "young man" until *after* the evil one has been overcome (see 1 John 2:12-14). This means your stress on settling the battles *within* is crucial!

As your Protégé worked through the material in Day 3 on pages 28-31, did God bring people to mind who need to be forgiven? Did the Protégé forgive these persons in prayer? Is there anyone who is very difficult to forgive? If there is a person that your Protégé is unwilling to forgive, ask if you can pray for them for God's heart of forgiveness.

Ask, "Do you recognize any strongholds in your life? Do you want freedom from them?" Be guided by your Protégé's response to these questions. Don't push or try to initiate ministry if there is not openness now. God's Spirit will continue to work in this area. If he or she wants freedom from some areas of bondage, arrange a time later in the week to meet and pray through these areas using the guidelines on pages 32-33. If the strongholds seem large and well rooted, you may want to ask your cell leader to join you or to recommend someone else to guide you in this ministry.

Explain that while Jesus has overcome Satan, the evil one will continually attempt to get a foothold in our lives. That is why God's armor and the empowering of the Holy Spirit are so important. Look at your Protégé's responses on page 35. If there is a real hunger for more of God's power, stop and pray for this for this new believer. When we thirst, God delights to give the overflowing presence of His Spirit to those who ask for Him (Luke 11:13).

4. PLAN YOUR NEXT GET-TOGETHER (5 MINUTES).

Clarify the time and place of your next meeting. As the mentor, you should begin today to get ready for your time together next week by reading the "Prepare for Your Time Together" section for Unit 4.

> *"I myself am convinced, my brothers, that you yourselves are full of goodness, complete in knowledge and competent to instruct one another."* Romans 15:14
>
> *"Let the word of Christ dwell in you richly as you teach and admonish one another with all wisdom, and as you sing psalms, hymns and spiritual songs with gratitude in your hearts to God." Colossians 3:16*
>
> *"Therefore encourage one another and build each other up, just as in fact you are doing." 1 Thessalonians 5:11*

UNIT 4 — FOLLOW JESUS AS LORD

PREPARE FOR YOUR TIME TOGETHER

1. Before this session, check with your cell leader to learn the proper procedures to prepare your Protégé for baptism. See what calendar date baptism could be scheduled for.

2. Review all the material in Unit 4 as well as the Scripture memory verses. Draw the heart illustrations on pages 38-39 on three separate pieces of paper before your session and take them with you to your time together. You will use these for your discussion of the unit.

3. Consider ways you can meet some of the people in the *oikos* of your Protégé. Express your desire to meet the family and friends that are important in his or her life. Make a visit to his or her home or possibly join in a social event-taking place this week. Be sensitive to those God may be drawing to Himself.

YOUR TIME TOGETHER

1. SHARE PERSONALLY WITH EACH OTHER (10 MINUTES).

Take your opening time this week to learn more about your Protégé's job. Where does this new believer work? Who is his or her boss? Discuss the expectation of employers in terms of work, obedience and loyalty.

2. REVIEW THE SCRIPTURE MEMORY VERSES (5 MINUTES)

Say together the first three memory verses:
- 1 John 5:11-12
- 1 Corinthians 10:13
- 1 John 1:9

Also go over your latest verse, John 16:24. If your Protégé is having trouble mastering the verses, discuss ways of finding more time to work on them such as reviewing them en route to work, when rocking a baby or when standing in line at a bank.

3. DISCUSS UNIT 4 ON FOLLOWING JESUS AS LORD (30 MINUTES).

Begin your discussion time by showing the Protégé the three heart illustrations from pages 38-39 that you have drawn on paper ahead of time. Ask the questions below:

"Which one of these best represented your life before becoming a Christian?"

"Which one best reflects your current relationship with Christ?"

If the new believer selects the diagram with both Jesus and Self on the throne, talk further about this. Be understanding. Perhaps he or she is being very honest, recognizing that at the present time Jesus is not fully on the throne. The condition may point to a stronghold. If your Protégé is ready to deal with it, set aside this week's study and spend the rest of your time praying through this, using the guidelines from pages 32-33.

If the Protégé selects the picture showing Christ alone as Lord, affirm this. Then ask, "What circumstances might make you choose the picture of the 'I' and 'Christ' sharing the throne? What would you do if that happened?"

Read Matthew 28:18-20 together from page 40, discussing the importance of following Jesus in baptism. Recall your earlier discussion about our employers' expectation of obedience. How much more should Jesus be able to expect our ready response to His instructions? That's why early Christians were baptized so quickly; they wanted to clearly declare Christ's Lordship over their lives. Discuss the procedures for baptism at your church and if your Protégé is ready, invite him or her to sign the form on page 41.

Look at the new believer's responses on page 43. This might pinpoint an area where God is inviting him or her to more fully yield to His lordship. Offer your prayer support to push through to victory.

If you have time, alternately read aloud the affirmations in Day 5 on "Know Who You Really Are!", page 45, putting the new believer's first name in each one. Ask your Protégé to read to you his or her "I am . . ." statement from the bottom of page 45.

4. PRAY AND MINISTER TO EACH OTHER (10 MINUTES).

5. PLAN YOUR NEXT GET-TOGETHER (5 MINUTES).

For your next time together, you will be taking some Listening Room time together. You may also want to have a little celebration to mark the end of this first study. For these reasons, you may want to meet at your home.

As mentor, you should begin today to get ready for your time together next week by reading the "Prepare for Your Time Together" section for Unit 5.

UNIT 5 — GROW IN GOD'S WORD

PREPARE FOR YOUR TIME TOGETHER

1. If the Protégé expressed a desire to be baptized, inform the cell leader and invite the new believer to share this with the cell group at your next cell meeting. Arrange a special celebration time in the cell group after the baptism has taken place.

2. Secure a copy of the next equipping or discipleship resource used in your church before this session or insure that the Protégé buys his or her own copy. It is important to build on the momentum of this current study to launch the next important phase of Christian growth. If you have not gone through this resource yourself, also secure a copy for yourself.

3. This unit will discuss different Bible translations and helps. You may want to bring several mentioned in the unit that you have found helpful to show your Protégé.

4. Prepare a meal or treat to share together as you conclude this study.

YOUR TIME TOGETHER

1. CELEBRATE THE COMPLETION OF THIS STUDY BY SHARING A MEAL OR TREAT TOGETHER (15 MINUTES).

2. REVIEW YOUR SCRIPTURE MEMORY (5 MINUTES).

Review together your previous verses: 1 John 5:11-12; 1 Corinthians 10:13; 1 John 1:9; and John 16:24.

Practice this week's verses together: 2 Corinthians 10:3-4 and Proverbs 3:5-6.

3. DISCUSS UNIT 5 ON GROWING IN GOD'S WORD (30 MINUTES).

Begin by relating the ways God has used His Word to shape and transform your life. You may want to share two or three of your favorite verses and what they have meant to you.

Briefly discuss the different versions of the Bible mentioned on pages 48-49. If your pastor or church uses one version predominantly, it may be best for this new believer to buy and use it when attending Celebrations.

How is your Protégé's Listening Room time coming along? Look at the responses given to the questions on page 50.

Discuss the Bible study tools listed in Day 4, pages 52-53.

Be sure to sign the "Verification of Completion" on page 55, congratulating the Protégé on the completion of this first study.

4. PLAN YOUR NEXT GET-TOGETHER (5 MINUTES).

Now is the time for you to give the new believer a copy of the next equipping resource that your church uses. Give your personal endorsement by sharing a lesson you learned through it that has impacted your life. You will Mentor your Protégé through this material just as you did through *Beginning the Journey*.

5. PRAY AND MINISTER TO EACH OTHER (10 MINUTES).

Congratulations! You have just completed a wonderful part of your own journey into ministry. Wasn't it a blessing to bless another person's life? Soon you will become *partners* in soul winning!

Week One

And this is the testimony: God has given us eternal life, and this life is in His Son. He who has the Son has life; he who does not have the Son of God does not have life.

1 John 5:11-12

Week Two

No temptation has seized you except what is common to man. And God is faithful; He will not let you be tempted beyond what you can bear. But when you are tempted, He will also provide a way out so that you can stand up under it.

1 Corinthians 10:13

Week Three

If we confess our sins, He is faithful and just and will forgive us our sins and purify us from all unrighteousness.

1 John 1:9

Week Four

Until now you have not asked for anything in My name. Ask and you will receive, and your joy will be complete.

John 16:24

Week Five

For though we live in the world, we do not wage war as the world does. The weapons we fight with are not the weapons of the world. On the contrary, they have divine power to demolish strongholds.

2 Corinthians 10:3-4

Week Five

Trust in the LORD with all your heart and lean not on your own understanding; in all your ways acknowledge Him, and He will make your paths straight.

Proverbs 3:5-6

REMOVE PAGE WITH SCISSORS ALONG THIS LINE

1 John 5:11-12

John 16:24

1 Corinthians 10:13

2 Corinthians 10:3-4

1 John 1:9

Proverbs 3:5-6